1000 FACTS ON
DINOSAURS

First published in 2002 by Miles Kelly Publishing Ltd
Bardfield Centre, Great Bardfield
Essex, U.K., CM7 4SL

This edition published by Barnes & Noble, Inc.

2 4 6 8 10 9 7 5 3

Editorial Director
Anne Marshall

Editors
Jenni Rainford, Nicola Sail

Design
WhiteLight

Americanization
Sean Connolly

Library of Congress Cataloging-in-Publication Data on file at the Library of Congress.

2004 Barnes & Noble Books

ISBN 0-7607-3751-7

Printed and bound in China

1000 FACTS ON
DINOSAURS

Steve Parker
Consultant: Dr. Jim Flegg

BARNES
&NOBLE
BOOKS
NEW YORK

Contents

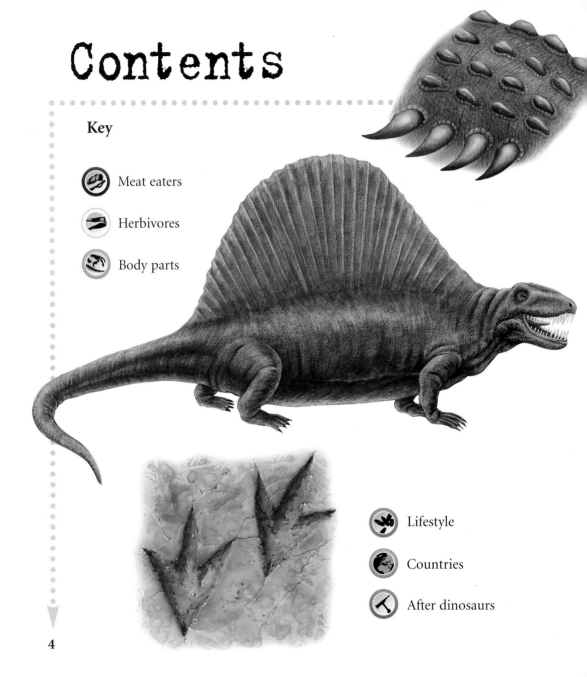

4

Contents

Contents

Contents

Ancestors

- **Experts have many opinions** as to which group (or groups) of reptiles were the ancestors of the dinosaurs.

- **The earliest dinosaurs** appeared in the Middle Triassic Period, about 230–225 million years ago, so their ancestors must have been around before this.

- **Very early dinosaurs** walked and ran on their strong back limbs, so their ancestors were probably similar.

- **The thecodonts** or "socket-toothed" group of reptiles may have been the ancestors of the dinosaurs.

▶ Thecodontosaurus *belonged to a group of reptiles that preceded the dinosaurs. It had a bulky body, long arms and walked on two legs. Like all the first dinosaurs, it was carnivorous.*

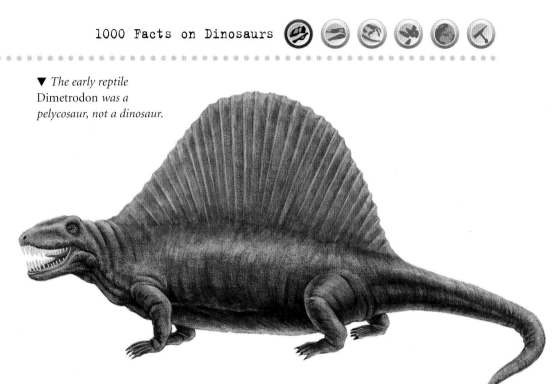

▼ *The early reptile*
Dimetrodon *was a*
pelycosaur, not a dinosaur.

- **A thecodont's** teeth grew from roots fixed into pitlike sockets in the jawbone, as in dinosaurs.

- **Some thecodonts** resembled sturdy lizards. Others evolved into true crocodiles (still around today).

- **The ornithosuchian thecodonts** became small, upright creatures with long back legs and long tails.

- **The smaller thecodonts** included *Euparkeria*, at about 2 ft (60 cm) long, and *Lagosuchus*, at about 1 ft (30 cm) long.

- *Euparkeria* **and** *Lagosuchus* were fast-moving creatures that used their sharp claws and teeth to catch insects.

Earliest dinosaurs

- **The first known dinosaurs** appeared about 230–225 million years ago, in the Middle Triassic Period.

- **The earliest dinosaurs** were small-to-medium meat eaters with sharp teeth and claws. They ran quickly on their two longer back legs.

- **Fossils of *Herrerasaurus*** date from 228 million years ago and were found near San Juan in Argentina, South America.

- ***Herrerasaurus* was about 10 ft (3 m)** in total length, and probably weighed some 200 lb (90 kg).

- **At about the same time and in the same place** as *Herrerasaurus*, there lived a similar-shaped dinosaur named *Eoraptor*, at only 5 ft (1.5 m) long.

  - **The name** *Eoraptor* means "dawn plunderer" or "early thief."

▲ Staurikosaurus *was one of the first dinosaurs, a fairly small carnivore measuring about 6 ft (2 m). It ran fast on two legs, using its long, stiff tail for balance.*

10

- *Staurikosaurus* **was a meat eater** similar to *Herrerasaurus*. It is known to have lived about the same time, in present-day Brazil, South America.

- *Procompsognathus* was another early meat eater. It lived in the Late Triassic Period in Germany.

- *Pisanosaurus* **lived in Argentina** in the Late Triassic Period, and was only 3 ft (1 m) long. It may have been a plant eater similar to *Lesothosaurus*.

> **FASCINATING FACT**
> *Eoraptor* and *Herrerasaurus* hunted small animals such as lizards, insects and mammal-like reptiles.

▲ Herrerasaurus *was one of the earliest carnivores, living about 230 million years ago. It moved on two powerful legs and its slim build, narrow head and sharp teeth and claws were similar to those of later meat eaters.*

Great meat eaters

...FASCINATING FACT....
Giganotosaurus lived about 100 million years
ago in today's Argentina, South America.

● **The large meat-eating dinosaurs**
belonged to a general group known as the
"carnosaurs."

● **All carnosaurs** were similar in body shape, and resembled the
fearsome *Tarbosaurus*.

● ***Tarbosaurus* was very similar** to *Tyrannosaurus*. It lived at the same
time, 70–65 million years ago, but in Asia rather than North America.

● **Some experts believe** that *Tarbosaurus* was an Asian version of the North
American *Tyrannosaurus*, and both should have been called *Tyrannosaurus*.

● **The carnosaur** *Albertosaurus* was about 27–30 ft (8–9 m)
long and lived 75–70 million years ago, in present-day
Alberta, Canada.

◄ Albertosaurus, *like the other carnosaurs, was a massive, powerful hunting
machine during the Cretaceous Period. It had clawed feet and hands, strong muscular
legs, razor sharp teeth, and a strong skull to protect it when attacking prey at speed.*

- *Spinosaurus* **was a huge carnosaur** from North Africa, measuring 40 ft (12 m) long and weighing 4–5 tons. It had tall, rodlike bones on its back, which may have been covered with skin, like a "sail."

- *Daspletosaurus* **was a 30-ft (9-m) long carnosaur** that lived at the end of the Age of Dinosaurs in Alberta, Canada.

- **Largest of all the carnosaurs** was *Giganotosaurus*, the largest meat eater ever to walk the Earth.

- *Giganotosaurus* was up to 53 ft (16 m) long and weighed at least 8 tons.

▶ *The Asian* Tarbosaurus *was almost identical to* Tyrannosaurus *with muscular legs walking on three clawed toes, tiny arms, and deep, powerful jaws.*

13

Tyrannosaurus

- *Tyrannosaurus* **is not only** one of the most famous of the dinosaurs, but also one about which a great deal is known. Several discoveries have revealed fossilized bones, teeth, whole skeletons, and other remains.

- *Tyrannosaurus* **lived at the very end** of the Age of Dinosaurs, about 68–65 million years ago.

- **The full name** of *Tyrannosaurus* is *Tyrannosaurus rex*, which means "king of the tyrant reptiles."

- **The head** of *Tyrannosaurus* was 4 ft (1.2 m) long and had more than 50 dagger-like teeth, some longer than 6 in (15 cm).

- *Tyrannosaurus* **fossils** have been found at many sites in North America, including Alberta and Saskatchewan in Canada, and Colorado, Wyoming, Montana, and New Mexico in the United States.

- **The arms and hands** of *Tyrannosaurus* were so small that they could not pass food to its mouth, and may have had no use at all.

- **Recent fossil finds** of a group of *Tyrannosaurus*, includes youngsters, suggesting that they may have lived as families in small herds.

- *Tyrannosaurus* **may have been** an active hunter, pounding along at speed after its fleeing prey, or it may have been a skulking scavenger that ambushed old and sickly victims.

- **Until the 1990s**, *Tyrannosaurus* was known as the biggest meat-eating animal ever to walk the Earth, but its size record has been broken by *Giganotosaurus*.

> **. . . FASCINATING FACT . . .**
> *Tyrannosaurus*, when fully grown, was about 40–43 ft (12–13 m) long. It weighed 6–7 tons.

▼ Tyrannosaurus's *powerful rear legs contrasted greatly with its puny front limbs or "arms." As it pounded along, its thick-based tail balanced its horizontal body and head, which was held low. The rear feet were enormous, with each set of three toes supporting some three or four tons.*

The huge skull of *Tyrannosaurus* was deep from top to bottom, but relatively narrow from side to side. The jaw hinged at the rear of the head, giving a vast gape when the mouth was open

Curved neck allowed head to face forward

Thick, heavy, muscular base to tail

Two-fingered "hand"

Deep chest probably gave great stamina

Three-toed foot

15

Allosaurus

▲ *Remains of up to 60* Allosaurus *were found here, at Dinosaur Quarry, Utah.* Allosaurus *fossils have also been found in Africa, where millions of years ago, there may have been a land bridge to North America.*

- ***Allosaurus* was a huge** meat-eating dinosaur, almost as big as *Tyrannosaurus.*

- ***Allosaurus*** was about 37–40 ft (11–12 m) in total length.

- **The weight** of *Allosaurus* is variously estimated at 1.5–4 tons.

- **The head** of *Allosaurus* was almost 3 ft (1 m) long, but its skull was light, with large gaps or "windows" that would have been covered by muscle and skin.

- ***Allosaurus* could not only** open its jaws in a huge gape, but it could also flex them so that the whole mouth became wider, for an even bigger bite.

▶ *The eyebrow "horns" of* Carnotaurus *are a puzzling feature. They do not seem large or strong enough to be weapons, and in any case, this dinosaur was already a very large and powerful creature. The horns may have grown with maturity, indicating that the owner was adult and able to breed.*

- **The name** *Carnotaurus* means "meat-eating bull," referring partly to its bulllike face.

- ***Carnotaurus* had two** curious, cone-shaped bony crests or "horns," one above each eye, where the horns of a modern bull would be.

- **Rows of extra-large scales**, like small lumps, ran along *Carnotaurus* from its head to its tail.

- **Like** *Tyrannosaurus, Carnotaurus* had very small front limbs that could not reach its mouth, and may have had no use.

- ***Carnotaurus* probably ate** plant-eating dinosaurs such as *Chubutisaurus*, although its teeth and jaws were not especially big or strong.

Pack hunters

- **Dinosaurs were reptiles**, but no reptiles today hunt in packs in which members cooperate with each other.

- **Certain types of crocodiles and alligators** come together to feed where prey is abundant, but they do not coordinate their attacks.

- **Fossil evidence** suggests that several kinds of meat-eating dinosaurs hunted in groups or packs.

- **Sometimes** the fossils of several individuals of the same type of dinosaur have been found in one place, suggesting the dinosaurs were pack animals.

- **The fossil bones** of some plant-eating dinosaurs have been found with many tooth marks on them, apparently made by different-sized predators, which may have hunted in packs.

- *Tyrannosaurus* may have been a pack hunter.

- **In southwest Montana,** the remains of three or four *Deinonychus* were found near the fossils of a much larger plant eater named *Tenontosaurus*.

- **A single** *Deinonychus* weighed 130–150 lb (60–70 kg), while *Tenontosaurus* weighed 15 times more.

- **One *Deinonychus*** probably would not have attacked a full-grown *Tenontosaurus*, but a group of three or four might have.

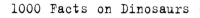

◀ *Slender, agile, and fast with sharp teeth and grasping claws,* Coelurus *was part of the coelurosaur group, small meat eaters that hunted lizards, insects, frogs, and small mammals. They may also have scavenged on the leftover prey of carnosaurs like* Allosaurus.

... FASCINATING FACT ...
Some meat eaters may have had fairly large brains, enabling them to hunt as a group.

Raptors

- **"Raptors"** is a nickname for the dromeosaur group.

- **"Raptor"** is variously said to mean "plunderer," "thief," or "hunter" (birds of prey are also called raptors).

- **Dromeosaurs** were medium-sized, powerful, agile, meat-eating dinosaurs that lived mainly about 110–65 million years ago.

- **Most dromeosaurs** were 5–10 ft (1.5–3 m) from nose to tail, weighed 45–135 lb (20–60 kg), and stood between 3–6 ft (1–2 m) tall.

- *Velociraptor* **lived** 75–70 million years ago, in what is now the barren scrub and desert of Mongolia in Central Asia.

▶ Velociraptor, *the "speedy thief," was a typical dromeosaur, with a sharp claw on each foot capable of cutting long gashes into its prey. Its fossils have been found in Central Asia.*

● **Like other raptors**, *Velociraptor* probably ran fast and could leap great distances on its powerful back legs.

  ● **The dromeosaurs** are named after the 6-ft (2-m) long *Dromeosaurus* from North America—one of the least known of the group, from very few fossil finds.

  ● **The best-known raptor** is probably *Deinonychus*.

  ● **The large mouths of dromeosaurs** opened wide and were equipped with many small, sharp, curved teeth.

> ...**FASCINATING FACT**...
> On each foot, a dromeosaur had a large, curved claw that it could swing in an arc to slash through its victim's flesh.

◀ Deinonychus, *in addition to its speed and agility when hunting, was able to leap up onto its prey, balanced by a rigid tail. The name* "Deinonychus" *means* "terrible claw."

Deinonychus

- *Deinonychus* **is one of the best-known** members from the group of meat eaters known as raptors.

- **The Middle Cretaceous Period**, about 115–100 million years ago, is when *Deinonychus* thrived.

- **Fossils of** *Deinonychus* come from the U.S. Midwest, mainly from Montana and Wyoming.

- *Deinonychus* **was about 10 ft (3 m) long** from nose to tail and weighed 130–155 lb (60–70 kg), about the same as an adult human.

- **When remains of** *Deinonychus* were dug up and studied in the 1960s, they exploded the myth that dinosaurs were slow, small-brained, and stupid.

- **Powerful, speedy, and agile,** *Deinonychus* may have hunted in packs, like today's lions and wolves.

- *Deinonychus* **had large hands** with three powerful fingers, each tipped with a dangerous sharp claw.

- **On each foot,** *Deinonychus* had a massive, scythelike claw that it could flick in an arc to slice open prey.

- **The tail** of *Deinonychus* was stiff and could not be swished.

- *Deinonychus* **and other similar** dromeosaurs, such as *Velociraptor*, were the basis for the cunning and terrifying raptors of the *Jurassic Park* films.

▶ Deinonychus *were dromeosaurs (meaning "swift reptile"). A combination of sharp teeth and claws and long, powerful legs for jumping onto prey made* Deinonychus *a powerful hunting machine. These dinosaurs hunted in packs and so were able to attack prey much larger than themselves.*

Oviraptor

- ***Oviraptor* was an unusual meat eater** from the dinosaur group known as theropods.

- **Fossils of** *Oviraptor* were found in the Omnogov region of the Gobi Desert in Central Asia.

- **From beak to tail tip**, *Oviraptor* was about 6 ft (2 m) long.

- ***Oviraptor* lived** during the Late Cretaceous Period about 85–75 million years ago.

▶ Oviraptor's *unusual features included a toothless, parrotlike beak and a hard, bony head crest. The crest may have been used to signify dominant members in a particular group or area.*

28

● **Oviraptor was named** "egg thief" because the first of its fossils was found lying among the broken eggs of another dinosaur, possibly *Protoceratops*.

● **The mouth of** *Oviraptor* had no teeth. Instead, it had a strong, curved beak, like that of a parrot or eagle.

● **On its forehead**, *Oviraptor* had a tall, rounded piece of bone, like a crest or helmet, sticking up in front of its eyes.

● *Oviraptor's* **bony head crest** resembled that of today's flightless bird, the cassowary.

● *Oviraptor* **may have eaten** eggs, or cracked open shellfish with its powerful beak.

◀ *The claws of the modern Australian cassowary are similar to those of the dromeosaurs. Cassowaries are shy forest dwellers but extremely aggressive if surprised. The long middle talon on each foot can inflict severe wounds and the bird itself can jump as high as 6 ft (2 m)!*

....FASCINATING FACT....
Oviraptor had two bony spikes inside its mouth that it may have used to crack eggs when it closed its jaws.

29

Dilophosaurus

◀ Dilophosaurus *had two crests on its head, although the fragile bone structure of these means that it is unlikely they were ever used for fighting rivals. Paleontologists (fossil experts) think it is possible that the crests were covered in brightly colored skin as a warning to rivals or for visual display.*

- *Dilophosaurus* was a large meat-eating dinosaur in the group known as the ceratosaurs.

- **About 200 million years ago**, *Dilophosaurus* roamed the Earth in search of prey.

- **Fossils** of *Dilophosaurus* were found in Arizona, and possibly Yunnan, China.

- **The remains** of *Dilophosaurus* in Arizona, were discovered by Jesse Williams, a Navajo Native American, in 1942.

- **Studying the fossils** of *Dilophosaurus* proved very difficult, and the dinosaur was not given its official name until 1970.

- *Dilophosaurus* **measured** about 20 ft (6 m) from its nose to the end of its very long tail.

> **FASCINATING FACT**
> *Dilophosaurus* probably weighed about 1,100 lb (500 kg)—as much as today's polar bears.

- **The name** *Dilophosaurus* means "two ridged reptile," from the two thin, rounded, bony crests on its head, each shaped like half a dinner plate.

- **The crests** of *Dilophosaurus* were too thin and fragile to be used as weapons for head-butting.

- **Brightly colored skin** may have covered *Dilophosaurus's* head crests, as a visual display to rivals or enemies.

▶ *The fearsome* Dilophosaurus *was one of the first large meat-eating dinosaurs. It gained the nickname "terror of the Early Jurassic."*

31

Baryonyx

▲ Baryonyx *had a large thumb claw on each hand. It may have been used when hunting lizards, fish, and amphibians, which formed the majority of its diet.*

- *Baryonyx* **was a large** meat-eating dinosaur that lived about 120 million years ago.

- **The first fossil find** of *Baryonyx* was its huge thumb claw, discovered in Surrey, England, in 1983.

- **The total length** of *Baryonyx* was 33–36 ft (10–11 m).

- *Baryonyx* **had a slim shape** and long, narrow tail, and probably weighed less than 2 tons.

- **The head** of *Baryonyx* was unusual for a meat-eating dinosaur in having a very long, narrow snout, similar to today's slim-snouted crocodiles.

- **The teeth** of *Baryonyx* were long and slim, especially at the front of its mouth.

- **The general similarities** between *Baryonyx* and a crocodile suggest that *Baryonyx* may have been a fish eater.

- ***Baryonyx* may have lurked** in swamps or close to rivers, darting its head forwards on its long, flexible neck to snatch fish.

- **The massive thumb claw** of *Baryonyx* may have been used to hook fish or amphibians from the water.

- **The long thumb claw** of *Baryonyx* measured about 14 in (35 cm) in length.

▲ *We only know of* Baryonyx *from a single fossil specimen. This was found alongside remains of fish scales, suggesting this dinosaur was a semiaquatic fish catcher. It had a straight neck, unlike may theropods, and narrow jaws containing 128 serrated teeth.*

Ornitholestes

Slim build for speedy, agile movement

- **Ornitholestes** was a smallish meat-eating dinosaur in the group known as coelurosaurs.

- **The name** *Ornitholestes* means "bird robber"—experts who studied its fossils in the early 1900s imagined it chasing and killing the earliest birds.

- **Ornitholestes** lived about 150 million years ago, at the same time as the first birds.

- **Present-day Wyoming** was the home of *Ornitholestes*, a continent away from the earliest birds in Europe.

- **Only one specimen** of *Ornitholestes* has been found, along with parts of a hand at another site.

Sharp claws for grasping prey

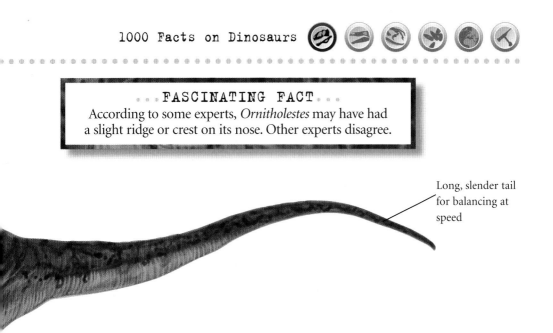

Long, slender tail for balancing at speed

- *Ornitholestes* **was** about 6 ft (2 m) long from nose to tail tip.

- **Slim and lightweight**, *Ornitholestes* probably weighed only about 26–33 lb (12–15 kg).

- **The teeth** of *Ornitholestes* were small and well spaced, but also slim and sharp, well suited to grabbing small animals for food.

  - *Ornitholestes* **had very strong** arms and hands, and powerful fingers with long claws, ideal for grabbing baby dinosaurs newly hatched from their eggs.

◀ Ornitholestes, *at 6 ft (2 m) long, had a very small body, with a long tail for balancing and long arms with clawed hands for grabbing its prey. It had a long snout and may have hunted in packs.*

35

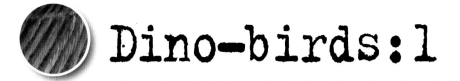

Flight feathers suited to agile maneuvers in the air

Teeth in long, light jaws

Three clawed "fingers" midway along front of wii

Long tail with tail backbones

▲ Archaeopteryx *could probably glide well, swoop and turn as it pursued flying prey such as dragonflies. However, its long, strong legs suggest that it was also an able walker and runner. So it may have chased victims such as baby lizards and cockroaches on the ground.*

36

> ...FASCINATING FACT...
> *Archaeopteryx* was covered with feathers
> that had the same detailed designs found
> in feathers covering flying birds today.

- **The earliest known bird** for which there is good fossil evidence, and which lived during the Age of Dinosaurs, is *Archaeopteryx*.

- *Archaeopteryx* **lived** in Europe during the Late Jurassic Period, about 155–150 million years ago.

- **At about 2 ft (60 cm) long** from nose to tail tip, *Archaeopteryx* was about the size of a large crow.

- *Archaeopteryx* **resembled** a small, meat-eating dinosaur in many of its features, such as the teeth in its long, beaklike mouth, and its long, bony tail.

- **In 1951**, a fossilized part-skeleton was identified as belonging to a small dinosaur similar to *Compsognathus*, but in the 1970s it was restudied and named *Archaeopteryx*—showing how similar the two creatures were.

- **Three clawed fingers** grew halfway along the front of each of *Archaeopteryx*'s wing-shaped front limbs.

- **The flying muscles** of *Archaeopteryx* were anchored to its large breastbone.

- *Archaeopteryx* **may have flown**, but not as skillfully as today's birds.

- *Archaeopteryx* **probably fed** by swooping on prey, running to catch small creatures such as insects and worms, or perhaps even by scavenging carrion.

Dino-birds:2

- **Fossils found during the last 20 years** show that some dinosaurs may have been covered with feathers or fur.

- *Sinosauropteryx* was a small, 3-ft (1-m) long meat eater that lived 135 million years ago in China.

- **Fossils** of *Sinosauropteryx* show that parts of its body were covered not with the usual reptile scales, but with feathers.

- **The overall shape** of *Sinosauropteryx* shows that, despite being feathered, it could not fly.

◀ Sinosauropteryx *was a small theropod dinosaur with a birdlike beak and featherlike structures on its body. The fossils were found in China, where similar discoveries have also been made. Did they move and behave like birds or like dinosaurs?*

▼ Avimimus *may have evolved feathers for warmth or for camouflage.*

- **The feathers** of *Sinosauropteryx* may have been for camouflage, for visual display, or to keep it warm—suggesting it was warm-blooded.

- *Avimimus* was a small, light dinosaur. Its fossils come from China and Mongolia, and date from 85–82 million years ago.

- **The 5-ft (1.5-m) long** *Avimimus* had a mouth shaped like a bird's beak for pecking at food.

- **The fossil arm bones** of *Avimimus* have small ridges of the same size and shape as the ridges on birds' wing bones, where feathers attach.

- **In modern science,** any animal with feathers is a bird, so some experts say that feathered dinosaurs were not actually dinosaurs or even reptiles, but birds.

- **Some experts say** that birds are not really a separate group of animals, but a subgroup of dinosaurs that lives on today, and they should be regarded as feathered dinosaurs.

Ostrich-dinosaurs

- **"Ostrich-dinosaurs"** is the common name of the ornithomimosaurs, because of their resemblance to today's largest bird—the flightless ostrich.

- **Ostrich-dinosaurs** were tall and slim, with two long, powerful back legs for very fast running.

- **The front limbs** of ostrich-dinosaurs were like strong arms, with grasping fingers tipped by sharp claws.

- **The eyes of ostrich-dinosaurs** were large and set high on the head.

- **The toothless mouth** of an ostrich-dinosaur was similar to the long, slim beak of a bird.

- **Ostrich-dinosaurs** lived towards the end of the Cretaceous Period, about 100–65 million years ago, in North America and Asia.

◀ At 6 ft (2 m) tall, Struthiomimus *was a similar height to a modern ostrich. In the legs, the bulk of the muscle was in the hips and upper thighs, as in an ostrich or horse—both rapid runners.*

- **Fossils of the ostrich-dinosaur** *Struthiomimus* from Alberta, Canada, suggest it was almost 13 ft (4 m) in total length and stood about 6 ft (2 m) tall—the same height as a modern ostrich.

- **The ostrich-dinosaur** *Gallimimus* was about 15 ft (5 m) in length and stood nearly 10 ft (3 m) high.

- **Ostrich-dinosaurs probably ate** seeds, fruits, and other plant material, as well as small animals such as worms and lizards, which they may have grasped with their powerful clawed hands.

- **Other ostrich-dinosaurs** included *Dromiceiomimus*, at 10–13 ft (3–4 m) long, and the slightly bigger *Ornithomimus*.

▶ Dromiceiomimus *was probably the fastest runner of its time, speeding along at 35–40 mph (60–70 km/h). The combination of large eyes and long, flexible neck gave good all-round visibility when it was hunting its prey.*

41

Eustreptospondylus

Slim, powerful
meat eater.

- *Eustreptospondylus* **was a large** meat eater that lived in present-day Oxfordshire and Buckinghamshire, in central southern England.

- *Eustreptospondylus* lived about 165 million years ago.

- **In the 1850s**, a fairly complete skeleton of a young *Eustreptospondylus* was found near Wolvercote, Oxford, but was named as *Megalosaurus*, the only other big meat eater known from the region.

▲ Eustreptospondylus *weighed about the same as a very large lion today, and was certainly just as deadly. We know about it from a single fossil find, in England, which was originally thought to be of* Megalosaurus, *another carnosaur.*

> **FASCINATING FACT**
> For more than 100 years, the fossil *Eustreptospondylus* from near Oxford was known by the name *Megalosaurus*.

- **In 1964,** British fossil expert Alick Walker showed that the Wolvercote dinosaur was not *Megalosaurus*, and gave it a new name, *Eustreptospondylus*.

- *Eustreptospondylus* means "well curved," or "true reversed, backbone."

  - **A full-grown** *Eustreptospondylus* measured about 23 ft (7 m) in total length.

- *Eustreptospondylus* is estimated to have weighed a massive 440–550 lb (200–250 kg).

  - **In its enormous mouth**, *Eustreptospondylus* had a great number of small, sharp teeth.

    - *Eustreptospondylus* **may have hunted** stegosaurs and also sauropods such as *Cetiosaurus*—both groups that roamed the region at the time.

      Fossil remains show similarities to the larger carnivore *Allosaurus*, which lived in North America some 10–15 million years later.

Smallest dinosaurs

- **One of the smallest dinosaurs** was *Compsognathus*, which lived during the Late Jurassic Period, 155–150 million years ago.

- **Fossils** of *Compsognathus* come from Europe, especially southern Germany and southeastern France.

- *Compsognathus* was slim, with a long, narrow tail. It probably weighed less than 6 lb (3 kg).

- **Each hand** of *Compsognathus* had two clawed fingers, and each foot had three long, clawed running toes, with another toe (the first or big toe) placed higher up in the "ankle" region.

- *Compsognathus* **had small teeth** that were sharp and curved. It probably darted through the undergrowth after insects, spiders, worms, and similar small prey.

- **Two other very small dinosaurs** were *Heterodontosaurus* and the 3-ft (1 m) long fabrosaur *Lesothosaurus*.

- **The smallest fossil dinosaur specimens** found to date are of *Mussaurus*, which means "mouse reptile."

- *Mussaurus* was a plant-eating prosauropod similar to *Plateosaurus*, which lived in the Late Triassic Period in South America.

- **The fossils of** *Mussaurus* measure just 8 in (20 cm) long—but these are the fossils of babies, just hatched from their eggs. The babies would have grown into adults measuring 10 ft (3 m) long.

▶ Compsognathus *was a carnivorous dinosaur and is relatively rare in terms of fossil finds. At 3 ft (1 m) long and about 6 lb (3 kg) in weight, it was one of the smallest dinosaurs, probably feeding on insects and small reptiles.* Compsognathus *was fast and agile but it is likely that it moved in packs for self-defense.*

...FASCINATING FACT...
The *Compsognathus* was only about 3 ft (1 m) long,
and some specimens were only 28 in (70 cm) long.

Herbivores

▶ *During the warm, damp Jurassic Period, there was lush plant life in most areas, covering land that had previously been barren. Massive plant eaters such as* Barosaurus *thrived on the high-level fronds, needles and leaves of towering tree ferns, gingkoes, and conifers.*

Barosaurus, 85 ft (26 m) long and 25–30 tons

- **Hundreds of kinds of dinosaur** were herbivores, or plant eaters. As time passed, the plants available for them to eat changed or evolved.

- **Early in the Age of Dinosaurs,** during the Triassic Period, the main plants for dinosaurs to eat were conifer trees, gingkoes, cycads, and the smaller seed-ferns, ferns, horsetails, and club mosses.

- **A few cycads** are still found today. They resemble palm trees, with umbrella-like crowns of long green fronds on top of tall, bare, trunklike stems.

- **In the Triassic Period**, only prosauropod dinosaurs were big enough or had necks long enough to reach tall cycad fronds or gingko leaves.

- **In the Jurassic Period**, tall conifers such as redwoods and "monkey puzzle" trees became common.

- **The huge, long-necked sauropods** of the Jurassic Period would have been able to reach high into tall conifer trees to rake off their needles.

- **In the Middle Cretaceous Period**, a new type of plant food appeared—the flowering plants.

- **By the end of the Cretaceous Period** there were many flowering trees and shrubs, such as magnolias, maples, and walnuts.

- **No dinosaurs ate grass**, because grasses did not appear on Earth until 30–20 million years ago, long after the dinosaurs had died out.

> . . . FASCINATING FACT . . .
> Gingkoes are still found today, in the form
> of maidenhair trees, with fan-shaped leaves.

Prosauropods

- **The prosauropods** were the first really big dinosaurs to appear on Earth. They were plant eaters that thrived about 230–180 million years ago.

- **Prosauropods** had small heads, long necks and tails, wide bodies and four sturdy limbs.

- **One of the first prosauropods** was *Plateosaurus*, which lived about 220 million years ago in present-day France, Germany, Switzerland, and other parts of Europe.

▶ *With their characteristic long necks and tails, the prosauropod group are thought to have preceded (come before) the sauropods. A member of this group,* Riojasaurus *was South America's first big dinosaur.*

- *Plateosaurus* usually walked on all fours, but it may have reared up on its back legs to reach high leaves.

- *Plateosaurus* was up to 26 ft (8 m) in total length, and weighed about 1 ton.

- **Another early prosauropod** was *Riojasaurus*. Its fossils are 218 million years old, and come from Argentina.

- *Riojasaurus* was 33 ft (10 m) long and weighed about 2 tons.

- *Anchisaurus* **was one of the smallest prosauropods,** at only 8 ft (2.5 m) long and about 65 lb (30 kg). It lived in eastern North America about 190 million years ago.

- **Fossil evidence** suggests that 16-ft (5-m) long *Massospondylus* lived in southern Africa and perhaps North America.

- **The sauropods** followed the prosauropods and were even bigger, but had the same basic body shape, with long necks and tails.

49

Plateosaurus

- *Plateosaurus*, a prosauropod, was one of the first really big dinosaurs to appear, some 220 million years ago.

- **The name** *Plateosaurus* means "flat reptile."

- **Groups of** *Plateosaurus* have been found at various sites, including one in Germany and one in France.

- *Plateosaurus* **used** its many small, serrated teeth to crop and chew plant food.

- *Plateosaurus* **had very flexible**, clawed fingers, which it perhaps used to pull branches of food to its mouth.

▼ *One of the earliest prosauropods,* Plateosaurus *may have reared up to chomp on leaves 6–10 ft (2–3 m) above the ground.*

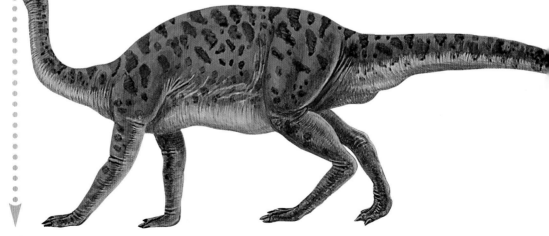

- *Plateosaurus* **could bend its fingers** "backward," allowing it to walk on its hands and fingers, in the same posture as its feet and toes.

- *Plateosaurus's* **thumbs** had especially large, sharp claws, perhaps used as weapons to jab and stab enemies.

- **Fossil experts** once thought that *Plateosaurus* dragged its tail as it walked.

- **Experts today** suggest that *Plateosaurus* carried its tail off the ground, to act as a balance to its head, long neck, and the front part of its body.

- *Plateosaurus* **was one of the earliest** dinosaurs to be officially named, in 1837, even before the term "dinosaur" had been invented.

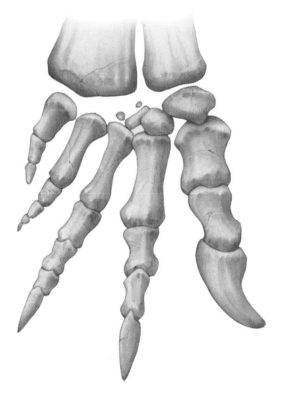

▲ *The front feet of* Plateosaurus *could be hyper-extended. The flexibility of the front feet meant that* Plateosaurus *may have been able to grasp branches when feeding.*

51

Biggest

- **The biggest dinosaurs** were the sauropods such as *Brachiosaurus* and *Argentinosaurus*—but working out how heavy they were when they were alive is very difficult.

- *Brachiosaurus* **is known** from many remains, including almost complete skeletons, so its length can be measured accurately.

- **A dinosaur's weight** is estimated from a scaled-down model of its skeleton "fleshed out" with muscles, guts and skin on the bones, using similar reptiles such as crocodiles for comparison.

- **The size of a dinosaur** model is measured by immersing it in water to find its volume.

- **The volume of a model dinosaur** is scaled up to find the volume of the real dinosaur when it was alive.

- **The sauropod** *Apatosaurus* is now well known from about 12 skeletons, which between them have almost every bone in its body.

- **Different experts** have "fleshed out" the skeleton of *Apatosaurus* by different amounts, so estimates of its weight vary from 20 tons to more than 50 tons.

▲ *It is thought that despite its massive size,* Apatosaurus *would have been able to trot surprisingly quickly on its relatively long legs.*

> ....FASCINATING FACT....
> The weights and volumes of reptiles alive today are used to calculate the probable weight of a dinosaur when it was alive.

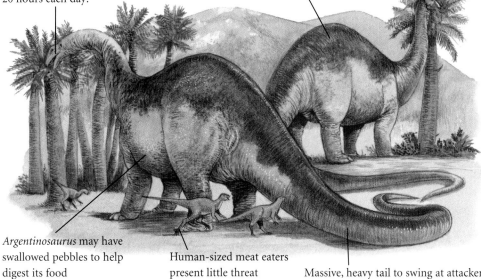

A small mouth meant that a large sauropod like *Argentinosaurus* would have had to feed for about 20 hours each day!

Reconstruction of *Argentinosaurus* is based on relatively few of its bones, compared with other bones from similar sauropod dinosaurs

Argentinosaurus may have swallowed pebbles to help digest its food

Human-sized meat eaters present little threat

Massive, heavy tail to swing at attackers

▲ Argentinosaurus *was a South American dinosaur, measuring up to 130 ft (39 m) long and weighing up to 110 tons. Despite this, fossil footprints show that some huge sauropods could run nearly as fast as a human!*

● **The length of** *Apatosaurus* is known accurately to have been 75 ft (23 m).

● **Fossils of a dinosaur called** *Brontosaurus* were found to be identical to those of *Apatosaurus*, and since the name *Apatosaurus* had been given first, this was the name that had to be kept—so, officially, there is no dinosaur called *Brontosaurus*.

53

Sauropods

- **The sauropods** were the biggest of all the dinosaurs.

- **The huge plant-eating sauropods** lived mainly during the Jurassic Period, 208–144 million years ago.

- **A typical sauropod** had a tiny head, a very long neck and tail, a huge, bulging body, and four massive legs, similar to those of an elephant, but much bigger.

- **Sauropods** included the well-known *Mamenchisaurus, Cetiosaurus, Diplodocus, Brachiosaurus,* and *Apatosaurus.*

▼ Apatosaurus *was a huge sauropod, but it may have been able to rear up on its back legs in order to defend itself or its young.*

▼ *For many years, the longest dinosaur known from fairly complete fossil remains was the sauropod* Diplodocus. *However, other dinosaurs, known from fewer fossils, may have been longer. An almost complete fossil skeleton of* Diplodocus, *found around 1900, has been copied many times in plaster, plastic, or fiberglass and sent to museums throughout the world.*

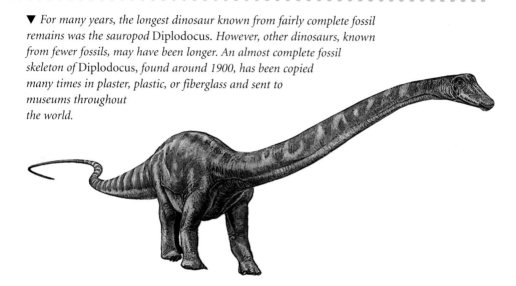

- *Rebbachisaurus fossils* were found in Morocco, Tunisia, and Algeria.

- *Rebbachisaurus lived* 120 million years ago.

- *Cetiosaurus* was about 60 ft (18 m) long and weighed 33 tons.

- *Cetiosaurus, or "whale reptile,"* was so named because French fossil expert Georges Cuvier originally thought that its giant backbones came from a prehistoric whale.

- *Cetiosaurus was the first* sauropod to be given an official name, in 1841—the year before the term "dinosaur" was invented.

- **The first fossils** of *Cetiosaurus* were discovered in Oxfordshire, England, during the 1830s.

Brachiosaurus

- **Relatively complete** fossil remains exist of *Brachiosaurus*.

- *Brachiosaurus* was a sauropod—a huge plant eater.

- **At 80 ft (25 m) long** from nose to tail, *Brachiosaurus* was one of the biggest of all dinosaurs.

- **Fossils** of *Brachiosaurus* have been found in North America, east and north Africa, and also possibly southern Europe.

- **Estimates of the weight** of *Brachiosaurus* range from about 30 to 75 tons.

- *Brachiosaurus* **lived** about 150 million years ago, and may have survived until 115 million years ago.

- **The name** *Brachiosaurus* means "arm reptile"—it was so named because of its massive front legs.

▼ Brachiosaurus *had similar body proportions to a giraffe, but was more than twice as tall and 50 times heavier.*

● **With its huge front legs** and long neck, *Brachiosaurus* could reach food more than 40 ft (12 m) from the ground.

● **The teeth** of *Brachiosaurus* were small and chisel-shaped for snipping leaves from trees.

● ***Brachiosaurus's*** nostrils were high on its head.

57

Diplodocus

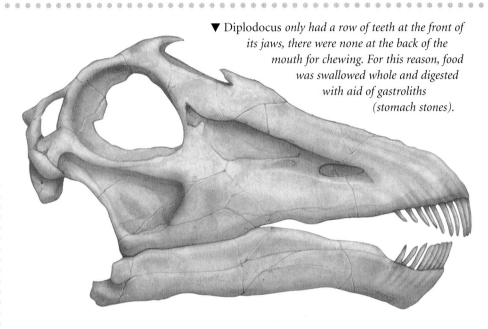

▼ Diplodocus *only had a row of teeth at the front of its jaws, there were none at the back of the mouth for chewing. For this reason, food was swallowed whole and digested with aid of gastroliths (stomach stones).*

- *Diplodocus* **was a huge plant-eating dinosaur** belonging to the group known as the sauropods.

- *Diplodocus* **lived** during the Late Jurassic Period, about 155–145 million years ago.

- **The first discovery** of *Diplodocus* fossils was in 1877, near Canyon City, Colorado.

- **The main fossils** of *Diplodocus* were found in Colorado, Utah, and Wyoming.

- **At an incredible 90 ft (27 m)** or more in length, *Diplodocus* is one of the longest known dinosaurs.

- **Although so long,** *Diplodocus* was quite lightly built—it probably weighed "only" 10–12 tons!

> . . . **FASCINATING FACT** . . .
> *Diplodocus's* nostrils were so high on its skull that experts once thought it had a trunk!

- *Diplodocus* probably swung its tiny head on its enormous neck to reach fronds and foliage in the trees.

- **The teeth** of *Diplodocus* were slim rods that formed a comblike fringe only around the front of its mouth.

- *Diplodocus* **may have used** its comblike teeth to strip leaves from twigs and swallow them without chewing.

◀ Diplodocus was long but light for a sauropod, weighing "only" about 10 tons. Like other sauropods, it used a combination of sheer size and a powerful whiplike tail to defend itself from predators.

59

Ankylosaurs

- **Ankylosaurs** had a protective armor of bony plates.

- **Unlike the armored nodosaurs**, ankylosaurs had a large lump of bone at the ends of their tails, which they used as a hammer or club.

- **One of the best-known ankylosaurs**, from the preserved remains of about 40 individuals, is *Euoplocephalus*.

- *Euoplocephalus*, **or "well-armored head,"** had bony shields on its head and body, and even had bony eyelids. Blunt spikes ran along its back.

- **The hefty** *Euoplocephalus* was 23 ft (7 m) long and weighed 2 tons or more.

▲ *"Ankylosaur" means "armored reptile" and* Ankylosaurus *most certainly was. Even its skull was protected by bony plates although it had a soft, vulnerable belly, so that it walked characteristically close to the ground.*

> ...FASCINATING FACT...
> *Pinacosaurus* was about 20 ft (6 m) long
> and lived in Asia 80–75 million years ago.

- *Euoplocephalus* lived about 75–70 million years ago in Montana and Alberta, Canada.

- **Specimens of** *Euoplocephalus* are usually found singly, so it probably did not live in herds.

- **The ankylosaur** *Pinacosaurus* had bony nodules like chain-mail armor in its skin, and rows of blunt spikes from neck to tail.

- **Ankylosaurs** had small, weak teeth, and probably ate soft, low-growing ferns and horsetails.

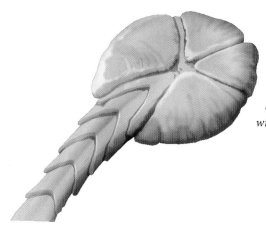

◀ *A powerful tail club was slow-moving* Ankylosaurus's *best weapon. It was made up of plates of fused bone and could be swung at an attacker with great force.*

Triceratops

▲ Triceratops *had a very short sturdy neck protected by a bony frill. In some ceratopsians (see Ceratopsians) however, the frill was simply very tough, bony skin which meant that it was a lot lighter.* Triceratops *moved in herds, giving it some protection from predators and was one of the last dinosaurs at the end of the Cretaceous Period.*

- **Many fossil remains** of *Triceratops* have been found. It is one of the most studied and best known dinosaurs.

- *Triceratops* **was the largest** of the plant-eating ceratopsians, the "horn-faced" dinosaurs.

- *Triceratops* **lived at the very end** of the Age of Dinosaurs, about 67–65 million years ago.

- **Fossils of 50 or so** *Triceratops* have been found in North America, though no complete skeleton has been found.

- *Triceratops* **was about 30 ft (9 m)** long and weighed 5–6 tons—as big as the largest elephants of today.

- **As well as a short nose horn** and two long eyebrow horns, *Triceratops* also had a wide, sweeping frill that covered its neck like a curved plate.

- **The neck frill** of *Triceratops* may have been an anchor for the dinosaur's powerful chewing muscles.

- **Acting as a shield,** the bony neck frill of *Triceratops* may have protected it as it faced predators head-on.

- *Triceratops'* **neck frill** may have been brightly colored, to impress rivals or warn off enemies.

- **The beaklike front** of *Triceratops'* mouth was toothless, but it had sharp teeth for chewing in its cheeks.

Fabrosaurs

- **Fabrosaurs** were small dinosaurs that lived toward the beginning of the Jurassic Period, about 208–200 million years ago.

- **The group was named** from *Fabrosaurus*, a dinosaur that was itself named in 1964, from just the fossil of a piece of lower jawbone, found in southern Africa.

▲ *On the outside,* Lesothosaurus *looked similar to small predatory dinosaurs such as* Compsognathus. *But its fossil teeth and jaws show that it was probably a plant eater, and an early member of the ornithischian group.*

- **Lesothosaurus was a fabrosaur**, the fossils of which were found in the Lesotho region of Africa, near the *Fabrosaurus* fossil. It was named in 1978.

- **The lightly built** *Lesothosaurus* was only 3 ft (1 m) long from nose to tail tip, and would have stood knee-high to an adult human.

- *Lesothosaurus* **had long, slim back legs** and long toes, indicating that it was a fast runner.

- **The teeth and other fossils** of *Lesothosaurus* show that it probably ate low-growing plants such as ferns.

- *Lesothosaurus's* **teeth** were set inwards slightly from the sides of its skull, suggesting it had fleshy cheek pouches for storing or chewing food.

- *Lesothosaurus* **may have** crouched down to rest on its smaller front arms when feeding on the ground.

- *Lesothosaurus* **probably lived in herds**, grazing and browsing, and then racing away at speed from danger.

- **Some experts believe** that *Lesothosaurus* and *Fabrosaurus* were the same, and that the two sets of fossils were given different names.

Mamenchisaurus

- *Mamenchisaurus* **was a massive** plant-eating dinosaur, a sauropod similar in appearance to *Diplodocus*.

- **The weight of** *Mamenchisaurus* has been estimated at 20–35 tons.

- *Mamenchisaurus* **lived** during the Late Jurassic Period, from about 160 to 140 million years ago.

- **The hugely long neck** of *Mamenchisaurus* had up to 19 vertebrae, or neckbones—more than almost any other dinosaur.

- *Mamenchisaurus* fossils were found in China.

- **The name** *Mamenchisaurus* is taken from the place where its fossils were discovered—Mamen Stream.

- *Mamenchisaurus* **had the longest neck**, at up to 50 ft (15 m), of any dinosaur yet discovered.

◀ *Over half of* Mamenchisaurus*'s length was its enormous neck! However, this was not balanced by a long tail, as in other sauropods like* Diplodocus *or* Brachiosaurus.

> ...**FASCINATING FACT**...
> *Mamenchisaurus* was a huge 80 ft
> (25 m) from nose to tail tip.

- ***Mamenchisaurus* may be a close cousin** of other sauropod dinosaurs found in the region, including *Euhelopus* and *Omeisaurus*.

- ***Mamenchisaurus* may have stretched** its vast neck high into trees to crop leaves, or—less likely—it may have lived in swamps and fed on soft, water-dwelling plants.

▲ *A skeleton of*
Mamenchisaurus's *head and neck.*
The muscles and the joints between each
pair of vertebrae would have been incredibly
strong, allowing Mamenchisaurus *to lift and lower its*
head and neck easily. In addition, the bones were hollow
to reduce the weight of the neck.

Heterodontosaurus

- *Heterodontosaurus* **was a very small dinosaur** at only 4 ft (1.2 m) in length (about as long as a large dog), and would have stood knee-high to a human.

- *Heterodontosaurus* lived about 205–195 million years ago, at the beginning of the Jurassic Period.

- **Probably standing partly upright** on its longer back legs, *Heterodontosaurus* would have been a fast runner.

- **Fossils** of *Heterodontosaurus* come from Lesotho in southern Africa and Cape Province in South Africa.

- **Most dinosaurs had teeth of only one shape** in their jaws, but *Heterodontosaurus* had three types of teeth.

▲ Heterodontosaurus *was a bipedal (two-legged), fast-moving, plant-eating dinosaur during the Early Jurassic Period (about 205 million years ago).*

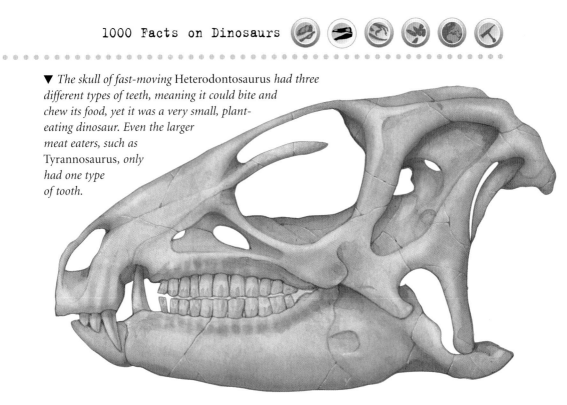

▼ *The skull of fast-moving* Heterodontosaurus *had three different types of teeth, meaning it could bite and chew its food, yet it was a very small, plant-eating dinosaur. Even the larger meat eaters, such as* Tyrannosaurus, *only had one type of tooth.*

- **The front teeth** of *Heterodontosaurus* were small, sharp and found only in the upper jaw. They bit against the horny, beaklike lower front portion of the mouth.

- **The four middle teeth** of *Heterodontosaurus* were long and curved, similar to the tusks of a wild boar, and were perhaps used for fighting rivals or in self-defense.

- **The back or cheek teeth** of *Heterodontosaurus* were long and had sharp tops for chewing.

- *Heterodontosaurus* **probably ate** low-growing plants such as ferns.

69

Duckbills

Possible inflatable bag of skin on snout and forehead

Tall, relatively narrow tail with muscular tail base to swish tail from side to side

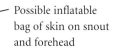

▲ *Fossil specimens of* Saurolophus *vary in size from about 30–40 ft (9–12 m). Its name means "ridged reptile" referring to the bony ridge on the top of its skull. It also had a ridge of bony projections along its back and tail, which looked almost like a long fin.*

Powerful rear legs for rapid walking and trotting

- "**Duckbills**" is the common name for the group of dinosaurs called the hadrosaurs.

- **Hadrosaurs were big plant eaters** that walked mainly on their two large, powerful rear legs.

- **Hadrosaurs** were one of the last main dinosaur groups to appear on Earth, less than 100 million years ago.

- **Hadrosaurs were named after** *Hadrosaurus*, the first dinosaur of the group to be discovered as fossils, found in 1858 in New Jersey.

- **Most hadrosaurs had wide mouths** that were flattened and toothless at the front, like a duck's beak.

- **Huge numbers of cheek teeth,** arranged in rows, filled the back of a hadrosaur's mouth. They were ideal for chewing tough plant food.

  - **Some hadrosaurs** had tall, elaborate crests or projections of bone on their heads, notably *Corythosaurus*, *Tsintaosaurus*, *Saurolophus* and *Parasaurolophus*.

    - **Hadrosaurs that lacked bony crests** and had low, smooth heads included *Anatosaurus*, *Bactrosaurus*, *Kritosaurus* and *Edmontosaurus*.

- **The name** *Hadrosaurus* means "big reptile."

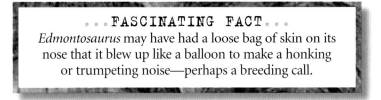

... FASCINATING FACT ...
Edmontosaurus may have had a loose bag of skin on its nose that it blew up like a balloon to make a honking or trumpeting noise—perhaps a breeding call.

Pachycephalosaurs

- **The pachycephalosaurs** are named after one of the best-known members of the group, *Pachycephalosaurus*.

- *Pachycephalosaurus* **means** "thick-headed reptile," due to the domed and hugely thickened bone on the top of its skull—like a bicycle helmet.

- **Pachycephalosaurs** were one of the last dinosaur groups to thrive. They lived 75–65 million years ago.

- **Pachycephalosaurs were plant eaters** that stood up and ran on their longer back legs.

- *Pachycephalosaurus* was about 15 ft (4.5 m) long from nose to tail, and lived in the U.S. Midwest.

- *Stegoceras*, also from the U.S. Midwest, was 8 ft (2.5 m) long with a goat-sized body.

Extra thick skull bone

◀ *Most of the pachycephalosaur group were quite small and at 27 ft (8 m)* Pachycephalosaurus *was certainly the largest. A solid dome of bone formed the top part of the skull—a protective element when fighting rivals. There were also spikes and nodules of bone decorating the head and face.*

72

- *Homalocephale*, **another pachycephalosaur**, was about 10 ft (3 m) long and had a flatter skull. It lived in east Asia.

- **Pachycephalosaurs** may have defended themselves by lowering their heads and charging at their enemies.

- **At breeding time**, the males may have engaged in head-butting contests, as some sheep and goats do today.

▲ Stegoceras *was a bipedal (two-legged) dinosaur, but since it moved with its back level, it is unlikely to have been capable of great speed. However, the stance would be useful when involved in head-butting fights with rivals.*

Stegosaurs

- **Stegosaurs** were a group of plant-eating dinosaurs that lived mainly during the Late Jurassic Period, 160–140 million years ago.

> **· · ·FASCINATING FACT· · ·**
> The back plates of *Kentrosaurus* were leaf- or diamond-shaped to about halfway along its back, and spike-shaped on its hips and tail.

- **Stegosaurs are named after** the best known of their group, *Stegosaurus*.

- **Stegosaurs are often called** "plated dinosaurs," from the large, flat plates or slabs of bone on their backs.

- **Stegosaurs** probably first appeared in eastern Asia, then spread to other continents, especially North America and Africa.

▼ Kentrosaurus *had an unusual defensive display—a combination of plates and spikes running the length of the body and tail. The "second brain" that was once thought to fill a space in a stegosaur's hip area is now known to have been a mass of nerves controlling the tail and back legs.*

74

▼ Stegosaurus *is thought to have had the smallest brain for its body size of all the dinosaurs, but the stegosaur group survived for more than 50 million years! It was a peaceful, slow-moving plant eater, so did not need the brain power of a fast hunter like Troodon.*

- **The stegosaur** *Kentrosaurus* was about 16 ft (5 m) long and weighed an estimated 1 ton.

- **The name** *Kentrosaurus* means "spiky reptile."

- *Kentrosaurus* lived about 155–150 million years ago in east Africa.

- **Most stegosaurs had no teeth** at the fronts of their mouths, but had horny beaks, like those of birds, for snipping off leaves.

- **Most stegosaurs chewed** their food with small, ridged cheek teeth.

Stegosaurus

The sails on the back may have been used for temperature control

The "beak" of *Stegosaurus* had no teeth—food was chewed with the cheek teeth

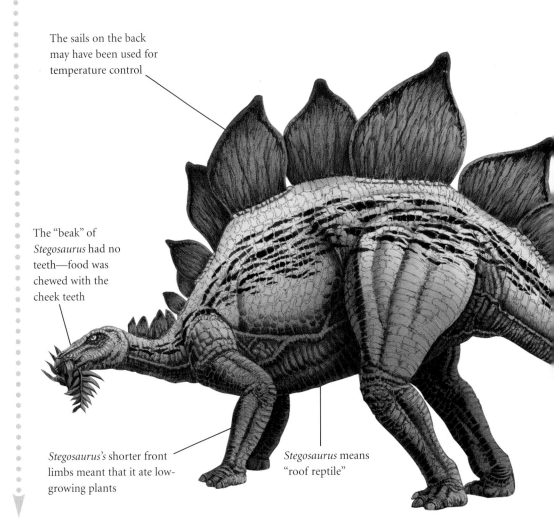

Stegosaurus's shorter front limbs meant that it ate low-growing plants

Stegosaurus means "roof reptile"

- *Stegosaurus* was the largest of the stegosaur group.

- **Fossils of** *Stegosaurus* were found mainly in present-day Colorado, Utah, and Wyoming.

- *Stegosaurus,* **like most of its group**, lived toward the end of the Jurassic Period, about 150 million years ago.

- **The mighty** *Stegosaurus* was about 27–30 ft (8–9 m) long from nose to tail tip and probably weighed more than 2 tons.

- **The most striking feature** of *Stegosaurus* was its large, roughly triangular bony plates along its back.

- **The name** *Stegosaurus* means "roof reptile." It was given this name because it was first thought that its 32-in (80-cm) long bony plates lay flat on its back, overlapping slightly like the tiles on a roof.

- **It is now thought** that the back plates of *Stegosaurus* stood upright in two long rows.

- **The back plates** of *Stegosaurus* may have been for body temperature control, allowing the dinosaur to warm up quickly if it stood side-on to the sun's rays.

- *Stegosaurus's* **back plates** may have been covered with brightly colored skin, possibly to intimidate enemies—they were too flimsy for protection.

- *Stegosaurus's* **tail** was armed with four large spikes, probably for swinging at enemies in self-defense.

The spiked tail would have delivered a powerful blow

Camarasaurus

- *Camarasaurus* **is one of the best known** of all big dinosaurs, because so many almost-complete fossil skeletons have been found.

- *Camarasaurus* was a massive plant-eating sauropod.

- *Camarasaurus* **lived** during the Late Jurassic Period, about 155–150 million years ago.

- **The famous American fossil-hunter** Edward Drinker Cope gave *Camarasaurus* its name in 1877.

- **The name** *Camarasaurus* means "chambered reptile," because its backbones, or vertebrae, had large, scoop-shaped spaces in them, making them lighter.

Large nostril and eye sockets

The name sauropod means "lizard footed"

- **The huge** *Camarasaurus* was about 60 ft (18 m) long.

- **Compared to other sauropods**, such as *Diplodocus*, *Camarasaurus* had a relatively short neck and tail, but a very bulky, powerful body and legs.

- **North America, Europe, and Africa** were home to *Camarasaurus*.

- **A large, short-snouted, tall head**, like that of *Brachiosaurus*, characterized the appearance of *Camarasaurus*.

- **A fossil skeleton** of a young *Camarasaurus* was uncovered in the 1920s, and had nearly every bone in its body lying in the correct position, as they were in life—an amazingly rare find.

◄ *Compared to other sauropods,* Camarasaurus *had a stocky body with a relatively short neck and tail.*

79

Ceratopsians

- **Ceratopsians** were large plant eaters that appeared less than 90 million years ago.

- **Most ceratopsian fossils** come from North America.

- **"Ceratopsian" means "horn-face,"** after the long horns on their snouts, eyebrows, or foreheads.

- **Most ceratopsians** had a neck shield or frill that swept sideways and up from behind the head to cover the upper neck and shoulders.

▶ Ceratopsians *were a group of dinosaurs with distinctive neck frills, horned faces, and parrot-like beaks. They had very powerful jaws, allowing them to feed on tough plants. It is likely that they moved in herds. A mass grave of ceratopsians unearthed in Canada contained at least 300 skeletons.*

▼ *Chasmosaurus*

▼ *Triceratops*

80

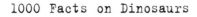

- **Well-known ceratopsians** included *Triceratops*, *Styracosaurus*, *Centrosaurus*, *Pentaceratops*, *Anchiceratops*, *Chasmosaurus*, and *Torosaurus*.

- **The neck frills of some ceratopsians**, such as that of *Chasmosaurus*, had large gaps or "windows" in the bone.

- **In life**, the windows in the neck frill of a ceratopsian were covered with thick, scaly skin.

- **Ceratopsians** had no teeth in the fronts of their hooked, beaklike mouths.

- **Using rows of powerful cheek teeth**, ceratopsians sheared their plant food.

▲ *Styracosaurus*

> ...FASCINATING FACT...
> *Torosaurus* had the longest skull of any land animal ever, at 8 ft (2.5 m) from the front of the snout to the rear of the neck frill.

81

Scelidosaurus

- *Scelidosaurus* **was a medium-sized** armored dinosaur, perhaps an early member of the group called the ankylosaurs.

- **Fossils of** *Scelidosaurus* have been found in North America, Europe, and possibly Asia.

- *Scelidosaurus* lived during the Early Jurassic Period, about 200 million years ago.

- **From nose to tail**, *Scelidosaurus* was about 13 ft (4 m) long.

- *Scelidosaurus* **probably moved about** on four legs, although it could perhaps rear up to gather food.

- **A plant eater**, *Scelidosaurus* snipped off its food with the beaklike front of its mouth, and chewed it with its simple, leaf-shaped teeth.

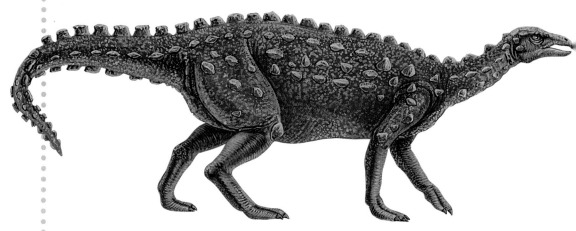

▲ Scelidosaurus *was a very widespread dinosaur that moved on all-fours and ate plants. It was a forerunner of the bigger, more heavily armored types.*

▶ Scelidosaurus *was covered from head to tail with hard scutes (bony plates in the skin) and nodules. These would have helped to protect it from meat-eating dinosaurs. It was a stocky, heavy-bodied dinosaur, which may have meant that it couldn't escape from predators very quickly.*

- *Scelidosaurus* is one of the earliest dinosaurs known to have had a set of protective, bony armor plates.

- **A row of about 50 bony plates**, or scutes, stuck up from *Scelidosaurus's* neck, back, and tail.

- *Scelidosaurus* had rows of conical bony plates along its flanks, resembling limpets on a rock.

- *Scelidosaurus* **was described in 1859**, and named in 1863, by Richard Owen, who also invented the name "dinosaur."

Anchisaurus

- *Anchisaurus* **was a prosauropod**, a plant eater with a small head, long neck, and long tail.

- **Although officially named as a dinosaur** in 1912, *Anchisaurus* had in fact been discovered almost 100 years earlier.

- *Anchisaurus* **was very small and slim** compared to other prosauropods, with a body about the size of a large dog.

- **Fossils** of *Anchisaurus* date from Early Jurassic times.

- **The remains of** *Anchisaurus* were found in Connecticut and Massachusetts, and in southern Africa.

- **With its small, serrated teeth,** *Anchisaurus* probably bit off the soft leaves of low-growing plants.

▼ Anchisaurus *was about the size of a large pet dog (such as a Labrador), but had a long neck and tail.*

- **To reach leaves** on higher branches, *Anchisaurus* may have been able to rear up on its back legs.

- *Anchisaurus* had a large, curved claw on each thumb.

- **The thumb claws of** *Anchisaurus* may have been used as hooks to pull leafy branches toward the mouth, and/or as weapons for lashing out at enemies and inflicting wounds.

▲ Anchisaurus *usually walked on all fours, but would have been able to rear up to feed or to run away quickly if in danger.*

.....FASCINATING FACT....
Anchisaurus fossils were discovered in North America in 1818, but at the time they were thought to be human remains!

Psittacosaurus

◀ Psittacosaurus *seemed to be an early member of the dinosaur
group known as the ceratopsians or horn-faces. It had the
characteristic birdlike beak, but had not yet evolved the face
horns or neck shield.* Psittacosaurus *was about the size of
a farmyard pig. Later members of the group would be
enormous, like* Triceratops.

86

- *Psittacosaurus* **was a plant eater** in the group known as the ceratopsians, or horn-faced dinosaurs.

- **Living in the Middle Cretaceous Period**, *Psittacosaurus* walked the Earth about 115–10 million years ago.

- *Psittacosaurus* was named in 1923 from fossils that were found in Mongolia, Central Asia.

- **Fossils** of *Psittacosaurus* have been found at various sites across Asia, including ones in Russia, China, and Thailand.

▲ *The beak of a modern-day parrot is similar to that of* Psittacosaurus. *The top jaw overlaps the bottom and can slice through tough plant material.*

- **The rear legs** of *Psittacosaurus* were longer and stronger than its front legs, suggesting that this dinosaur may have reared up to run fast on its rear legs, rather than running on all four legs.

- *Psittacosaurus* measured about 6 ft (2 m) in length.

- **On each foot** *Psittacosaurus* had four toes.

- **The name** *Psittacosaurus* means "parrot reptile," after the dinosaur's beak-shaped mouth, like that of a parrot.

- **Inside its cheeks,** *Psittacosaurus* had many sharp teeth capable of cutting and slicing through tough plant material.

Massospondylus

- *Massospondylus* was a medium-sized plant eater belonging to the group known as the prosauropods.

- **Africa and perhaps North America** were home to *Massospondylus*, about 200 million years ago.

- **In total**, *Massospondylus* was about 16 ft (5 m) long, with almost half of this length being its tail.

- **The rear legs** of *Massospondylus* were bigger and stronger than its front legs, so it may have reared up to reach high-up food.

▶ *The tiny head of* Massospondylus *would be kept busy, gathering food to fuel the bulky body. It may have spent 20 hours feeding each day! As with the other sauropods, it digested its food with the help of gastroliths (swallowed stones).*

- **The name** *Massospondylus* means "huge backbone."

- **Fossils of more than 80** *Massospondylus* have been found, making it one of the best-studied dinosaurs.

- *Massospondylus* **had a tiny head** compared to its large body, and it must have spent many hours each day gathering enough food to survive.

- **The front teeth** of *Massospondylus* were surprisingly large and strong for a plant eater, with ridged edges more like meat-eating teeth.

- **The cheek teeth** of *Massospondylus* were too small and weak for chewing large amounts of plant food, so perhaps the dinosaur's food was mashed mainly in its stomach.

- **In the 1980s**, some scientists suggested that *Massospondylus* may have been a meat eater, partly because of the ridged edges on its front teeth.

89

Tuojiangosaurus

- *Tuojiangosaurus* was a member of the group we know as the plated dinosaurs, or stegosaurs.

- **The first nearly complete dinosaur skeleton** to be found in China was of a *Tuojiangosaurus*, and excellent fossil skeletons are on display in several Chinese museums.

- **The name** *Tuojiangosaurus* means "Tuo River reptile."

- *Tuojiangosaurus* lived during the Late Jurassic Period, about 155 million years ago.

- *Tuojiangosaurus* was 23 ft (7 m) long from nose to tail tip.

- **The weight of** *Tuojiangosaurus* was probably about 1 ton.

- **Like other stegosaurs**, *Tuojiangosaurus* had tall slabs or plates of bone on its back.

- **The back plates of** *Tuojiangosaurus* were roughly triangular and probably stood upright in two rows that ran from the neck to the middle of the tail.

- *Tuojiangosaurus* **plucked low-growing plant food** with the beak-shaped front of its mouth, and partly chewed the plant material with its leaf-shaped, ridge-edged cheek teeth.

▶ Tuojiangosaurus *was a stegosaur, a group of heavily armored, small-brained herbivores that survived for over 50 million years. Stegosaurs' main defense was their tail. It could deliver a powerful blow with cone-shaped plates on the underside and long wounding spikes at the end.*

> ···· **FASCINATING FACT** ····
> *Tuojiangosaurus* had four long tail spikes,
> arranged in two Vs, which it could swing
> at enemies to keep them at a distance.

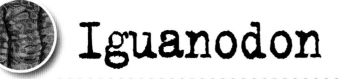

Iguanodon

● *Iguanodon* **was a large plant eater** in the dinosaur group known as ornithopods.

● **Numerous fossils** of *Iguanodon* have been found in several countries in Europe, including England, Belgium, Germany, and Spain.

● *Iguanodon* measured about 30 ft (9 m) from nose to tail.

● **A large elephant today**, at 4–5 tons, is estimated to weigh about the same as *Iguanodon* did.

● *Iguanodon* **lived** during the Early to Middle Cretaceous Period, 140–110 million years ago.

● *Iguanodon* **probably walked** and ran on its large, powerful back legs for much of the time, with its body held horizontal.

▲ *When a fossil of the thumb spike was first unearthed, paleontologists thought it belonged on* Iguanodon's *nose!*

▶ *Herbivorous* Iguanodon *may have used its large thumb spike as defense against enemies. It would have delivered a nasty stab wound to the neck or flank.*

- **A cone-shaped spike** on *Iguanodon*'s thumb may have been a weapon for jabbing at rivals or enemies.

- **The three central fingers** on *Iguanodon*'s hands had hooflike claws for four-legged walking.

- **The fifth or little finger** of *Iguanodon* was able to bend across the hand for grasping objects, and was perhaps used to pull plants toward the mouth.

◀ Iguanodon *had claws on its feet. But these were rounded and blunt and looked more like hoofs.*

93

Nodosaurs

▶ *Nodosaurids,*
like Polacanthus, *were*
quite primitive in
comparison with the
other ankylosaurs. They
lacked the bony tail club of
the ankylosaurids but still
had formidable protective
armor in the form of
plates and spikes
embedded into their
tough skin.

- **Nodosaurs** were a subgroup of armored dinosaurs, in the main ankylosaur group.

- **The nodosaur subgroup** included *Edmontonia, Sauropelta, Polacanthus,* and *Nodosaurus.*

- **Nodosaurs were slow-moving**, heavy-bodied plant eaters with thick, heavy nodules, lumps, and plates of bone in their skin for protection.

- **Most nodosaurs lived** during the Late Jurassic and the Cretaceous Periods, 150–65 million years ago.

- *Edmontonia* **lived in North America** during the Late Cretaceous Period, 75–70 million years ago.

- *Edmontonia* **was about 23 ft (7 m) long**, but its bony armor made it very heavy for its size, at 4–5 tons.

- **Along its neck, back and tail** *Edmontonia* had rows of flat and spiky plates.

- **The nodosaur** *Polacanthus* was about 13 ft (4 m) long and lived 120–110 million years ago.

- **Fossils** of *Polacanthus* come from the Isle of Wight, southern England, and from South Dakota.

▲ *Nodosaurids were part of the ankylosaur group of dinosaurs. Their bodies were protected with spikes and plates but they did not have a tail club. Like all armored dinosaurs, they had soft, vulnerable bellies and so moved quite close to the ground.*

. . . .**FASCINATING FACT**. . . .
Like many nodosaurs, *Edmontonia* and *Polacanthus* probably had long, fierce spikes on their shoulders, used to "spear" enemies.

95

Segnosaurs

- **Little is known** about the segnosaur group of dinosaurs—the subject of much disagreement among experts.

- **Segnosaurs are named after** almost the only known member of the group, Segnosaurus.

▼ Segnosaurus *is one of those dinosaurs that we just don't know that much about. Scientists have grouped it with the sauropods, but it has some unusual additional features! Instead of having four stocky legs, it may have moved around quite easily on two legs, using its clawed front feet to feed. We do know that it ate plants, but it may have eaten meat as well which no other sauropod did.*

▶ *Another unusual feature of*
Segnosaurus *was that it was not*
typically lizard-hipped.

- **The name Segnosaurus** means "slow reptile."

- **Segnosaurus lived** during the Mid to Late Cretaceous Period, about 90 million years ago.

- **Fossils of Segnosaurus** were found mainly in the Gobi Desert in Central Asia in the 1970s. The dinosaur was named in 1979 by Mongolian scientist Altangerel Perle.

- **Segnosaurus had a narrow head** and probably a toothless, beaklike front to its mouth.

- **Experts** have variously described Segnosaurus as a predatory meat eater, a swimming or wading fish eater, a rearing-up leaf eater, or even an ant eater.

- **Different experts** have said Segnosaurus was a theropod, a prosauropod, and an ornithopod.

- **Some scientists have suggested** that Segnosaurus was a huge dinosaur-version of today's anteater—ripping open the nests of termites and ants with its powerful claws.

97

Sauropelta

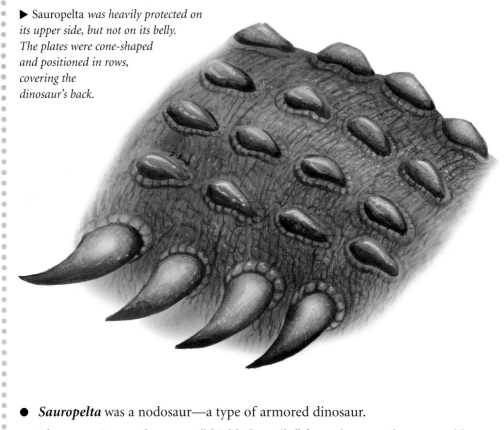

▶ Sauropelta *was heavily protected on its upper side, but not on its belly. The plates were cone-shaped and positioned in rows, covering the dinosaur's back.*

- **Sauropelta** was a nodosaur—a type of armored dinosaur.

- **The name** *Sauropelta* means "shielded reptile," from the many large, conelike lumps of bone—some almost as big as dinner plates—on its head, neck, back, and tail.

- **The larger lumps of bone** on *Sauropelta* were interspersed with smaller, fist-sized bony studs.

...FASCINATING FACT...
Sauropelta lived 110–100 million years ago,
in present-day Montana and Wyoming.

- *Sauropelta* **had a row of sharp spikes** along each side of its body, from just behind the eyes to the tail. The spikes decreased in size towards the tail.

- *Sauropelta* **was about 25 ft (7.5 m) long**, including the tail, and its bulky body and heavy, bony armor meant it probably weighed almost 3 tons.

- **The armor** of *Sauropelta* was flexible, almost like lumps of metal set into thick leather, so the dinosaur could twist and turn, but was unable to run very fast.

- **Strong, sturdy, pillar-like legs** supported *Sauropelta's* great weight.

- *Sauropelta* probably defended itself by crouching down to protect its softer belly, or swinging its head to jab at an enemy with its long neck spines.

- **Using its beak-like mouth**, *Sauropelta* probably plucked at low-growing plant food.

▶ Sauropelta *was an armored dinosaur with bony plates on its back and sides and a stiff tail. It was large and stocky, but lacked the defensive advantage of a tail club.*

Monsters

▼ *Only discovered in the 1980s,* Giganotosaurus *was a South American dinosaur. At 50 ft (15 m) long, it may well have been the biggest ever meat-eating dinosaur—bigger than* Tyrannosaurus! *Its short thigh bone may mean that it moved at a similar speed to* Tyrannosaurus *when pursuing prey.*

- **Dinosaurs** can be measured by length and height, but "biggest" usually means heaviest or bulkiest.

- **Dinosaurs were not the biggest-ever living things** on Earth—some trees are more than 100 times their size.

- **The sauropod dinosaurs** of the Late Jurassic were the biggest animals to walk on Earth, as far as we know.

- **Sauropod dinosaurs** may not have been the biggest animals ever. Today's great whales, and perhaps the massive, flippered sea reptiles called pliosaurs of the Dinosaur Age, rival them in size.

- **For any dinosaur**, enough fossils must be found for a panel of scientists to be sure it is a distinct type, so they can give it a scientific name. They must also be able to estimate its size. With some giant dinosaurs, not enough fossils have been found.

- *Supersaurus* **remains** found in Colorado, suggest a dinosaur similar to Diplodocus, but perhaps even longer, at 115 ft (35 m).

- *Seismosaurus* **fossils** found in 1991 in the United States may belong to sauropod up to 130 ft (40 m) long.

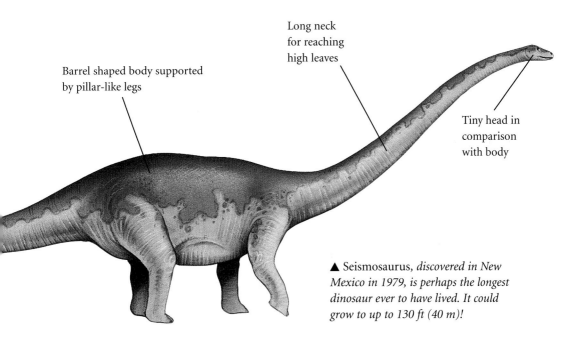

Long neck for reaching high leaves

Barrel shaped body supported by pillar-like legs

Tiny head in comparison with body

▲ Seismosaurus, *discovered in New Mexico in 1979, is perhaps the longest dinosaur ever to have lived. It could grow to up to 130 ft (40 m)!*

101

Myths

▶ Dimorphodon *was one of the early pterosaurs,*
190 million years ago. Attached to the wings were
large clawed hands while powerful legs indicate that
they were used for walking and running.
Dimorphodon *had a large head in comparison*
to its body, with a deep mouth and sharp teeth
for eating small reptiles and fish.

- **Dinosaurs were the only animals alive** during the Age of Dinosaurs—false, there were many kinds of creatures, from worms, insects, and fish to other kinds of reptiles.

- **Dinosaurs flew in the air**—false, although other reptiles called pterosaurs did fly.

- **Dinosaurs lived in the sea**—false, although other reptiles such as ichthyosaurs and plesiosaurs did.

- **Mammals appeared** on Earth after the dinosaurs died out—false. Small mammals lived all through the Age of Dinosaurs.

- **A single kind of dinosaur** survived all through the Age of Dinosaurs—false. A few kinds may have lived for 10, 20, or even 30 million years, but none came close to 160 million years.

- **Dinosaurs were huge** lizards—false. Dinosaurs were reptiles, but not members of the lizard group.

- **Dinosaurs gave birth to babies**—false. As far as we know, all species of dinosaur laid eggs.

- **All dinosaurs** were green—false, probably.
- **Dinosaurs live on today**—false … unless you've found one!

> ...**FASCINATING FACT**...
> Dinosaurs and humans fought each other—
> false. The last dinosaurs died out more than
> 60 million years before humans appeared.

◀ Plesiosaurus *was one of many plesiosaurs that thrived in Jurassic seas. However, it was not a dinosaur, as dinosaurs could neither fly nor live in the sea. Some people think that the Loch Ness Monster is a living relative of these prehistoric sea creatures!*

Male and female

- **In many living reptiles,** females are larger than males.

- **In dinosaur fossils,** the shapes of the hip bones and head crests can indicate if the creatures were male or female.

- **Head crest fossils** of different sizes and proportions belonging to the hadrosaur (duck-billed dinosaur) *Lambeosaurus* have been found.

- **Some** *Lambeosaurus* had short, rounded main crests with small, spikelike spurs pointing up and back.

- **Other** *Lambeosaurus* had a large, angular main crest with a large spur pointing up and back.

- **The head crest differences** in *Lambeosaurus* fossils may indicate that males and females looked different.

- **Remains of the hadrosaur** *Corythosaurus* show two main sizes of head crest, perhaps one belonging to females and the other to males.

- **New studies** in the variations of head crests led to more than eight different species of dinosaurs being reclassified as one species of *Corythosaurus*.

- **In dinosaurs and other animals,** differences between the sexes—either in size or specific features—is known as sexual dimorphism.

Head crest size may indicate if a hadrosaur was male or female.

····FASCINATING FACT····
In *Parasaurolophus* specimens, some
head crests were twice as long as others
—probably a male–female difference.

◀ Lambeosaurus *was a member of the*
hadrosaur group. The hollow crest on its
head could have identified the dominant
dinosaur in a particular area or
indicated male and female
members to other members
of a group. It could even
have been used for
calling to each
other during the
mating season.

105

Dinosaur eyes

◀ Troodon *had one of the largest brains, for its body size, of any dinosaur.* Troodon's *skull also had very large eye cavities, indicating that it had correspondingly large eyes, suitable for hunting at night.*

- **No fossils have been found of dinosaur eyes**, because eyes are soft and squishy, and soon rot away after death, or are eaten by scavengers.

- **The main clues** to dinosaur eyes come from the hollows, or orbits, in the skull where the eyes were located.

- **The orbits** in fossil dinosaur skulls show that dinosaur eyes were similar to those of reptiles today.

- **The 20-ft (6-m) long sauropod** *Vulcanodon* had tiny eyes in relation to the size of its head.

- **Small-eyed dinosaurs** probably only had good vision in the daytime.

- **The eyes** of many plant-eating dinosaurs, such as *Vulcanodon*, were on the sides of their heads, giving them all-round vision.

- **The small meat eater** *Troodon* had relatively large eyes, and it could probably see well even in dim light.

● *Troodon's* **eyes** were on the front of its face and pointed forward, allowing it to see detail and judge distance.

● **Dinosaurs that had large bulges**, called optic lobes, in their brains —detectable by the shapes of their skulls—could probably see very well, perhaps even at night.

◄ *Few dinosaurs had eyes as large, in comparison to the proportions of the whole head, as* Leaellynasaura. *They rival the size of the eyes of today's day-time birds.*

107

Noses

▲ Ornithomimus *had nasal openings near the tip of its beak, unlike the nostrils of a modern bird.*

- **Dinosaurs breathed** through their mouths and/or noses, like many other creatures today.

- **Fossil dinosaur skulls** show that there were two nose openings, called nares, in the bone.

- **A dinosaur's two nasal openings**, or nares, led to nasal chambers inside the skull, where the smell organs were located.

- **Some meat eaters**, especially carnosaurs such as *Allosaurus* and *Tyrannosaurus*, had very large nasal chambers and probably had an excellent sense of smell.

▶ Tyrannosaurus *had very large nasal cavities which indicates to scientists that it had a very good sense of smell.*

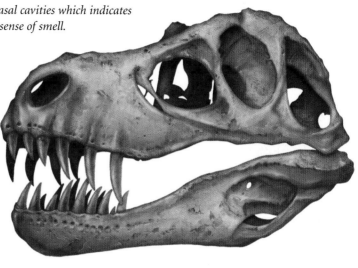

- **In most dinosaurs** the nasal opening were at the front of the snout, just above the upper jaw.

- **In some dinosaurs**, especially sauropods such as *Mamenchisaurus* and *Brachiosaurus,* the nasal openings were higher on the skull, between the eyes.

- **Fossils** show that air passages led from the nasal chambers rearward into the head for breathing.

· · · FASCINATING FACT · · ·
In hadrosaurs, the nasal passages were more than 3 ft (1 m) long.

- **The nasal openings** in a dinosaur's skull bone led to external openings, or nostrils, in the skin.

- **New evidence** from animals alive today suggests that a dinosaur's nostrils would have been lower down than the nares (the openings in the skull bone), toward the front of the snout.

Horns

◀ *The structure of a dinosaur horn was made up of two parts: an inner core and an outer protective covering. This is similar to the composition of horns in modern mammals, such as antelope.*

> **...FASCINATING FACT...**
> Dinosaurs may have used their horns to push over plants or dig up roots for food.

- **A dinosaur's horns** got bigger as the animal grew—they were not shed and replaced each year—just like the antlers of today's deer.

- **Each horn** had a bony core and an outer covering of a horny substance formed mainly from keratin.

- **Horns** were most common among the plant-eating dinosaurs. They were probably used for self-defense and to defend offspring against predators.

- **The biggest horns** belonged to the ceratopsians or "horn-faced" dinosaurs, such as *Triceratops*.

- **In some ceratopsians**, just the bony core of the horn was about 3 ft (1 m) long, not including the outer sheath.

- **The ceratopsian** *Styracosaurus* or "spiked reptile" had a series of long horns around the top of its neck frill, and a very long horn on its nose.

- **Horns may have been used** in head-swinging displays to intimidate rivals and make physical fighting less likely.

- **In battle**, male dinosaurs may have locked horns in a trial of strength, as antelopes do today.

- **Armored dinosaurs** such as the nodosaur *Panoplosaurus* had hornlike spikes along the sides of its body.

▼ *Like other ceratopsians,* Styracosaurus' *frill had a formidable row of horns which formed part of the dinosaur's defense. The frill horns had bony centers, which meant that they weighed heavily on the neck.*

Beaks

▲ Some reconstructions of Parasaurolophus *show a "web" of skin extending from the bony head crest, and curving down to the back of the neck. The skin could have been brightly colored in life, perhaps part of a visual display for mating, herd dominance or gaining territory.*

- **Several kinds of dinosaurs** had a toothless, beak-shaped front to their mouths.

- **Beaked dinosaurs** included ceratopsians (horn-faces) such as *Triceratops*, ornithopods such as *Iguanodon* and the hadrosaurs (duckbills), stegosaurs, segnosaurs, ankylosaurs (armored dinosaurs), and fast-running ostrich-dinosaurs.

- **Most beaked dinosaurs** had chopping or chewing teeth near the backs of their mouths, in their cheeks, but ostrich-dinosaurs had no teeth.

- **A dinosaur's beak** was made up of the upper (maxilla) and the lower (mandible) jaw bones.

- **Ornithischian (bird-hipped) dinosaurs** had what is called a "predentary" bone at the front tip of the lower jaw.

- **Ceratopsian (horn-faced) dinosaurs** had a "rostral" bone at the front tip of the upper jaw.

- **In life,** the bones at the front of a dinosaur's jaw would have been covered with horn, which formed the outer shape of the beak.

- **Dinosaurs almost certainly** used their beaks for pecking, snipping, tearing, and slicing their food.

- **Dinosaurs may have** used their beaks to peck fiercely at any attackers.

> ...**FASCINATING FACT**...
> Some of the largest beaks in relation to body size belonged to *Oviraptor* and *Psittacosaurus*.

▼ Protoceratops *was the first in the ceratopsian group of dinosaurs. It had a small frill that protected its neck area and a tough beak for cropping vegetation.*

113

Teeth

▼ Edmontosaurus *had hundreds of teeth packed together in its upper and lower jaws for grinding its diet of conifer needles, fruit and leaves.*

- **Some of most common fossil remains** of dinosaurs are their teeth—the hardest parts of their bodies.

- **Dinosaur teeth** come in a huge range of sizes and shapes—daggers, knives, shears, pegs, combs, rakes, filelike rasps, crushing batteries, and vices.

- **In some dinosaurs**, up to three quarters of a tooth was fixed into the jaw bone, so only one quarter showed.

- **The teeth of plant eaters** such as *Iguanodon* had angled tops that rubbed past each other in a grinding motion.

- **Some duckbill dinosaurs** (hadrosaurs) had more than 1,000 teeth, all at the back of the mouth.

▶ *The shape, number, and layout of teeth within the jawbones are clear evidence for what a dinosaur ate. Meat eaters like* Baryonyx *and* Tyrannosaurus *had huge sharp teeth for tearing through the flesh of their prey. Some plant eaters like* Apatosaurus *had no chewing teeth at all!*

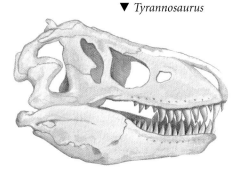

▲ *Baryonyx*

▼ *Apatosaurus*

- **Like modern reptiles**, dinosaurs probably grew new teeth to replace old, worn or broken ones.

- **Individual teeth** were replaced at different times.

- **Some of the largest teeth** of any dinosaur belonged to 30-ft (9-m) long *Daspletosaurus*, a tyrannosaur-like meat eater.

- **Some of** *Daspletosaurus's* teeth were up to 7 in (18 cm) long.

▼ *Tyrannosaurus*

. . . **FASCINATING FACT** . . .
Troodon, or "wounding tooth," was named on the evidence of just one or two teeth.

115

Stomach stones

- **Some dinosaur fossils** are found with unusually smooth, rounded stones, like seashore pebbles, jumbled up among or near them.

- **Smoothed pebbles** occur with dinosaur fossils far more than would be expected by chance alone.

- **Smooth stones** are mainly found with or near the remains of large plant-eating dinosaurs, especially those of prosauropods such as *Massospondylus*, *Plateosaurus*, and *Riojasaurus*, sauropods such as *Brachiosaurus* and *Diplodocus*, the parrot-beaked *Psittacosaurus,* and the stegosaurs.

- **Some plant-eating dinosaurs** may have used smooth stones to help process their food.

▶ *Dinosaurs in the sauropod group, like* Barosaurus, *did not chew their food before swallowing. Instead, they swallowed stones which ground up the food in a part of the digestive system called the gizzard. This meant that they wasted no time when feeding their huge bodies!*

116

- **The smoothed pebbles** associated with dinosaur remains are known as gastroliths, gastric millstones, or gizzard stones.

- **Gastroliths** were stones that a dinosaur found on the ground and deliberately swallowed into its stomach.

- **In the dinosaur's stomach**, gastroliths acted as "millstones," crushing and churning plant food, and breaking it down into a soft pulp for better digestion.

- **As gastroliths churned and rubbed** inside a dinosaur's guts, they became very rounded, smoothed and polished.

- **Gastroliths as small as a pea** and as large as a basketball have been found.

- **Gastroliths may be the reason why** many big plant eaters, especially sauropods, had no chewing teeth—the mashing was done inside the guts.

▶ *Gastroliths vary in size from smaller than grapes to larger than basketballs. They have been found adjacent to many dinosaur fossil finds.*

117

Legs and posture

▶ The small plant eater Hypsilophodon *was a bipedal dinosaur, walking and running on its two larger back legs.*

- **All dinosaurs had four limbs.** Unlike certain other reptiles, such as snakes and slow worms, they did not lose their limbs through evolution.

- **Some dinosaurs**, such as massive, plant-eating sauropods like *Janenschia*, stood and walked on all four legs nearly all the time.

- **The all-fours method** of standing and walking is called "quadrupedal."

- **Some dinosaurs**, such as nimble, meat-eating dromeosaurs like *Deinonychus*, stood and walked on their back limbs only. The front two limbs were used as arms.

- **The back-limbs-only method** of standing and walking is called "bipedal."

- **Some dinosaurs**, such as hadrosaurs like *Edmontosaurus*, could move on all four limbs or just on their back legs if they chose to.

- **Today, the only reptiles** that have an almost upright posture are crocodiles and alligators. They can only keep it up for a few seconds though as they gallop along in their "high walk."

- **Reptiles** such as lizards and crocodiles have a sprawling posture, in which the upper legs join the body at the sides.

- **Dinosaurs** had an upright posture, with the legs directly below the body.

- **The more efficient upright posture** and gait may be one major reason why dinosaurs were so successful compared to other animals of the time.

▶ Dromeosaurus *was slim and agile, making it a fast, effective hunter. It ran on two legs, possibly hunting in packs and this combination meant that it could probably prey on much larger animals.*

119

Hips

- **All dinosaurs are classified** in one of two large groups, according to the design and shape of their hip bones.

- **One of the two large groups of dinosaurs** is the Saurischia, which means "lizard-hipped."

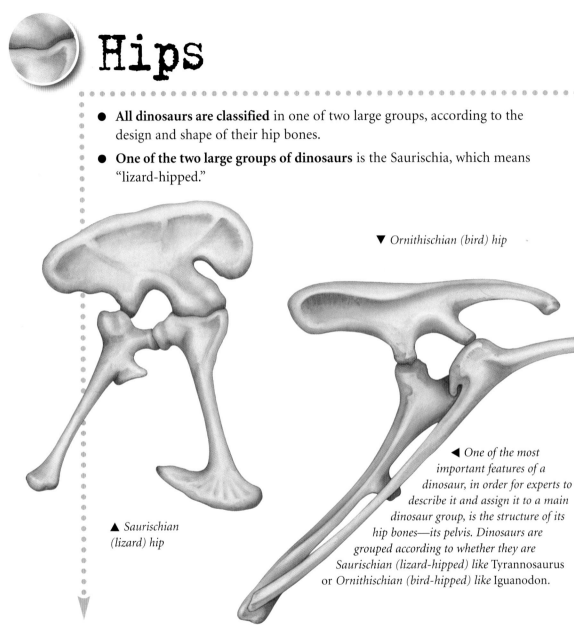

▼ *Ornithischian (bird) hip*

▲ *Saurischian (lizard) hip*

◄ *One of the most important features of a dinosaur, in order for experts to describe it and assign it to a main dinosaur group, is the structure of its hip bones—its pelvis. Dinosaurs are grouped according to whether they are Saurischian (lizard-hipped) like Tyrannosaurus or Ornithischian (bird-hipped) like Iguanodon.*

- **In a saurischian dinosaur**, the lower front pair of rod-shaped bones in the pelvis project down and forwards.

- **All meat-eating dinosaurs** belonged to the Saurischia.

- **The biggest dinosaurs**, the plant-eating sauropods, belonged to the Saurischia group.

- **The second of the two groups of dinosaurs** is the Ornithischia, meaning "bird-hipped."

- **In an ornithischian dinosaur**, the lower front pair of rod-shaped bones in the pelvis, called the pubis bones, project down and backward, lying parallel with another pair, the ischium bones.

- **All dinosaurs** in the group Ornithischia, from small *Heterodontosaurus* to huge *Triceratops*, were plant eaters.

- **In addition to hips,** there are other differences between the Saurischia and Ornithischia, such as an "extra" bone called the predentary at the front tip of the lower jaw in ornithischians.

> **...FASCINATING FACT...**
> The lizard-hipped design of meat eaters
> was better at anchoring leg muscles,
> which made them fast runners.

Claws

- **Like reptiles today**, dinosaurs had claws or similar hard structures at the ends of their digits (fingers and toes).

- **Dinosaur claws** were probably made from keratin—the same hard substance that formed their horns, and from which our own fingernails and toenails are made.

- **Claw shapes and sizes** relative to body size varied greatly between dinosaurs.

- **In many meat-eating dinosaurs** that ran on two back legs, the claws on the fingers were long and sharp, similar to a cat's claws.

- **A small, meat-eating dinosaur** such as *Troodon* probably used its finger claws for grabbing small mammals and lizards, and for scrabbling in the soil for insects and worms.

- **Larger meat-eating dinosaurs** such as *Allosaurus* may have used their hand claws to hold and slash their prey.

- **Huge plant-eating sauropods** such as *Diplodocus* had claws on its elephant-like feet that resembled nails or hoofs.

- **Many dinosaurs** had five clawed digits on their feet, but some, such as *Tyrannosaurus*, had only three toes on each foot to support their weight.

- **Some of the largest dinosaur claws** belonged to *Deinocheirus*—its massive finger claws were more than 14 in (35 cm) long.

- ***Deinocheirus* was probably** a gigantic ostrich-dinosaur that lived in the Late Cretaceous Period in Mongolia. Only parts of its fossil hands and arms have been found, so the rest of it remains a mystery.

▶ Troodon *may have been the best-equipped dinosaur hunter ever. It had a bigger brain than most and its large eyes may have been useful for hunting at night. Troodon's long, lethal claws would have enabled it to grab and hold prey while running at speed.*

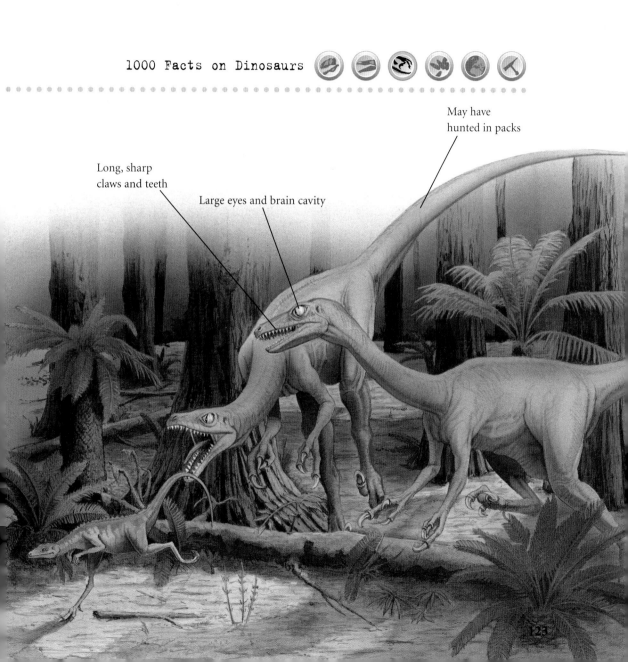

May have
hunted in packs

Long, sharp
claws and teeth

Large eyes and brain cavity

Skin

- **Several fossils of dinosaur skin** have been found, revealing that dinosaurs had scales, like today's reptiles.

- **As in crocodiles**, the scales of a dinosaur were embedded in its thick, tough, leathery hide, rather than lying on top of its skin and overlapping, as in snakes.

- **When the first fossils** of dinosaur skin were found in the mid-1800s, scientists thought they were from giant prehistoric crocodiles.

- **Fossil skin** of the horned dinosaur *Chasmosaurus* has been found.

▼ *Specific dinosaur markings like those seen on this reconstruction of* Corythosaurus *can only be guessed at. Scientists use information from the skin colors and textures of living reptiles such as lizards to predict what dinosaur colors and markings might have looked like.*

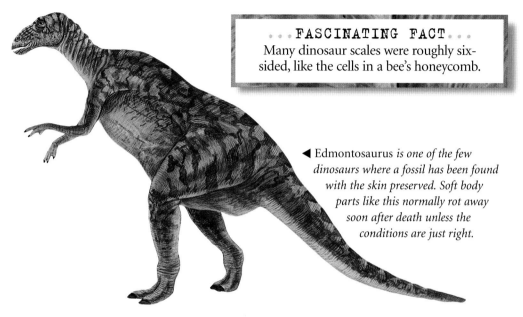

> ···**FASCINATING FACT**···
> Many dinosaur scales were roughly six-sided, like the cells in a bee's honeycomb.

◄ Edmontosaurus *is one of the few dinosaurs where a fossil has been found with the skin preserved. Soft body parts like this normally rot away soon after death unless the conditions are just right.*

- *Chasmosaurus* **had larger bumps or lumps**, called tubercles, scattered among its normal-sized scales.

- **Samples of fossil skin** belonging to the duckbill hadrosaur *Edmontosaurus* have been found.

- *Edmontosaurus* **was covered** in thousands of small scales, like little pebbles, with larger lumps or tubercles spaced among them.

- **Various specimens** of fossil skin show that the scales of *Iguanodon*-type dinosaurs were larger than those of same-sized, similar duckbill dinosaurs.

- **Scaly skin** protected a dinosaur against the teeth and claws of enemies, accidental scrapes, and the bites of small pests such as mosquitoes and fleas.

125

Armor

- **Many kinds of dinosaurs** had protective "armor."

- **Some armor** took the form of bony plates, or osteoderms, embedded in the skin.

- **A dinosaur with armor** might weigh twice as much as a same-sized dinosaur without armor.

- **Armored dinosaurs** are divided into two main groups—the ankylosaurs and the nodosaurs.

- **The large sauropod** *Saltasaurus* had a kind of armor.

- *Saltasaurus* **had hundreds** of small, bony lumps, each as big as a pea, packed together in the skin of its back.

- **On its back**, *Saltasaurus* also had about 50 larger pieces of bone the size of a human hand.

- *Saltasaurus* **is named after** the Salta region of Argentina, where its fossils were found.

- **Uruguay** provided another site for *Saltasaurus* fossils.

- *Saltasaurus* **was 40 ft (12 m) long** and weighed about 3–4 tons.

▶ *Ankylosaurus's tail club was nearly 3 ft (1 m) across and could deliver a crippling blow to an unsuspecting predator. In addition to this, the back and head were protected by large bony lumps and plates.*

A predator such as *Spinosaurus* would need to attack *Ankylosaurus* very carefully!

Ankylosaurus's hefty tail club could deliver a painful blow

127

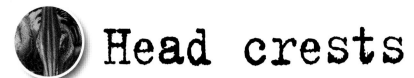

Head crests

▲ Parasaurolophus *may have used the hollow tubes inside its long head crest to make sounds. The tubes ran from the nose to the end of the crest. These sounds may have been used to identify themselves or as warnings of danger.*

- **Many dinosaurs** had lumps, bumps, plates, bulges, ridges, or other shapes of bone on their heads, called head crests.

> **...FASCINATING FACT...**
> The head crests of some large *Parasaurolophus*, perhaps full-grown males, reached an incredible 6 ft (2 m) in length.

- **Head crests** may have been covered with brightly colored skin in life, for visual display.

- **Meat eaters with head crests** included *Carnotaurus* and *Dilophosaurus*.

- **The dinosaurs with the largest** and most complicated head crests were the hadrosaurs.

- **The largest dinosaur head crest** was probably a long, hollow, tubular shape of bone belonging to the hadrosaur *Parasaurolophus*.

- **The head crests of hadrosaurs** may have been involved in making sounds.

- **Some years ago** the hadrosaur *Tsintaosaurus* was thought to have a very unusual head crest—a hollow tube sticking straight up between the eyes, like a unicorn's horn.

- **The so-called head crest** of *Tsintaosaurus* is now thought to be the fossil part of another animal, and not part of *Tsintaosaurus* at all.

- *Tsintaosaurus* is now usually known as *Tanius*, a hadrosaur with a small crest or no crest at all!

129

Sails

- **Long, bony extensions**, like rods or spines, stuck up from the backs of some dinosaurs.

- **In life**, a dinosaur's bony extensions may have held up a large area of skin, commonly called a back sail.

- **Dinosaurs with back sails** included the huge meat eater *Spinosaurus* and the large plant eater *Ouranosaurus*.

▶ *The predator* Spinosaurus *was almost as large as* Tyrannosaurus. *Its sail would have been about 6 ft (2 m) tall.*

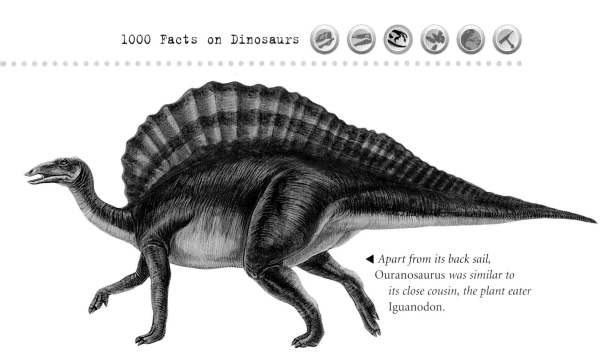

◀ *Apart from its back sail,* Ouranosaurus *was similar to its close cousin, the plant eater* Iguanodon.

- *Spinosaurus* **and** *Ouranosaurus* both lived 100 million years ago.
- **Fossils of** *Spinosaurus* and *Ouranosaurus* were found in North Africa.
- **The skin** on a dinosaur's back sail may have been brightly colored, or may even have changed color, like the skin of a chameleon lizard today.
- **A dinosaur's back sail** may have helped to control its body temperature.
- **Standing sideways** to the sun, a back sail would absorb the sun's heat and allow the dinosaur to warm up quickly, ready for action.
- **Standing in the shade**, a back sail would lose warmth and help the dinosaur to avoid overheating.
- **The bony back rods** of *Spinosaurus* were up to 5 ft (1.5 m) tall.

131

Dinosaur feet

▶ *Even though they were almost certainly slow-moving beasts, the splay-toed feet of sauropods were cushioned, much like the feet of elephants today.*

- **Dinosaur feet differed**, depending on the animal's body design, weight, and general lifestyle.

- **A typical dinosaur's front feet** had metacarpal bones in the lower wrist or upper hand, and two or three phalangal bones in each (finger or toe), tipped by claws.

- **The rear feet** of a typical dinosaur had metatarsal (instead of metacarpal) bones in the lower ankle.

- **Some dinosaurs had five toes** per foot, like most other reptiles (and most birds and mammals).

- **Sauropods** probably had feet with tough, rounded bases supported by a wedge of fibrous, cushion-like tissue.

> **FASCINATING FACT**
> The dinosaur group that includes all the meat eaters, large and small, is named the theropods, or "beast feet."

- **Most sauropods** had claws on their first three toes, and smaller, blunter "hoofs" on the other two toes.

- **Ostrich-dinosaurs** such as *Gallimimus* had very long feet and long, slim toes for fast running.

- **Many fast-running dinosaurs** had fewer toes, to reduce weight—*Gallimimus* had three toes per back foot.

- **The dinosaur group** that includes *Iguanodon*, duck-billed dinosaurs, *Heterodontosaurus,* and many other plant eaters is named the ornithopods, or "bird feet."

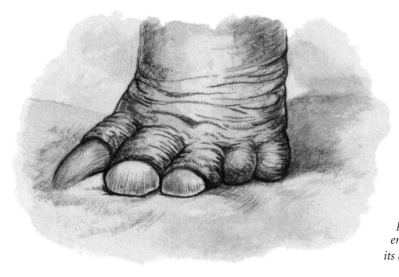

◄ Apatosaurus *was a massive beast, but could trot surprisingly quickly on its relatively long legs. It had a sharp, 7-in (17-cm) claw on each front foot, possibly to protect it from enemies or to help it to balance its huge frame.*

133

Footprints

- **Thousands of fossilized dinosaur** footprints have been found. They are located all over the world.

- **Some dinosaurs left footprints** when they walked on the soft mud or sand of riverbanks. Then the mud baked hard in the sun, and was covered by more sand or mud, which helped preserve the footprints as fossils.

- **Some fossil footprints** were made when dinosaur feet left impressions in soft mud or sand that was then covered by volcanic ash, which set hard.

- **Many footprints** have been found together in lines, called "trackways." These suggest that some dinosaurs lived in groups, or used the same routes regularly.

- **The distance between same-sized footprints** indicates whether a dinosaur was walking, trotting or running.

▶ *This footprint shows that* Tyrannosaurus *walked on the tips of its toes as opposed to on flat feet like most large dinosaurs. Each foot would have supported about 3–4 tons in weight.*

134

▶ *Many fossil footprints of similar shapes but different sizes, some overlapping, show a herd of mixed size and varying age passed this way. The relative positions of footprints indicate how the dinosaur was standing or moving.*

- **Footprints of big meat eaters** such as *Tyrannosaurus* show three toes with claws, on a forward-facing foot.

- **In big plant eaters** such as *Iguanodon*, each footprint shows three separate toes, but less or no claw impressions, and the feet point slightly inward.

- **In giant plant-eating sauropods**, each footprint is rounded and has indentations of nail-like "hoofs."

- **Some sauropod footprints** are more than 3 ft (1 m) across.

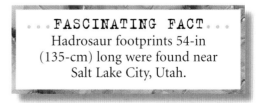

...**FASCINATING FACT**...
Hadrosaur footprints 54-in (135-cm) long were found near Salt Lake City, Utah.

135

Tails

▶ Hadrosaurus, *like other dinosaurs in the hadrosaur group, was a peaceful herbivore. It had a tall, narrow tail, similar to that of a modern crocodile. This may have helped it to maneuver its body in water, although predominantly, it lived on land.*

- **All dinosaurs** evolved with tails—though some individuals may have lost theirs in attacks or accidents!

- **The length of the tail** relative to the body, and its shape, thickness and special features, give many clues as to how the dinosaur used it.

- **The longest tails,** at more than 56 ft (17 m), belonged to the giant plant-eating sauropods such as *Diplodocus*.

- **Some sauropods** had a linked chain of more than 80 separate bones inside the tail—more than twice the usual number.

- **A sauropod** may have used its tail as a whip to flick at enemies.

- **Many meat-eating dinosaurs** that stood and ran on their back legs had thick-based tails to counterbalance the weight of their bodies and heads.

- **Small, fast, agile meat eaters**, such as *Compsognathus*, used their tails for balance when leaping and darting about.

- **The meat eater** *Ornitholestes* had a tail that was more than half of its 6-ft (2-m) length, and was used as a counterbalance-rudder to help it turn corners at speed.

- **The armored dinosaurs** known as ankylosaurs had two huge lumps of bone at the ends of their tails, which they swung at their enemies like a club.

- **The tails of the duck-billed dinosaurs** (hadrosaurs) may have been swished from side to side in the water as an aid to swimming.

▶ Compsognathus *had a long stiff tail that helped it to balance and turn quickly when it was running fast.*

137

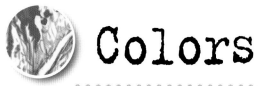

Colors

- **No one knows** for certain what colors dinosaurs were.

- **There are several good fossil specimens** of dinosaur skin, but all of them are stone colored, because fossils are living things that have turned to stone.

- **Some experts believe** that dinosaurs were similar in color to crocodiles—dull greens and browns.

- **Dinosaurs** that were dull greens and browns would have been well camouflaged among trees, rocks, and earth.

- **According to some experts**, certain dinosaurs may have been bright yellow, red, or blue, and could even have been striped or patched, like some of today's lizards and snakes.

- **Some dinosaurs** may have been brightly colored to frighten off predators or to intimidate rivals at breeding time.

▶ *The back plates of stegosaurs were probably used for heat regulation. However, they could also have been used for display purposes.*

▶ *Colorful images like this one of* Giganotosaurus *are no more than fanciful guesses—scientists just don't know what color dinosaurs were because there is no evidence. Certain body parts, such as sails and head crests, may have been brightly colored to attract mates or scare rivals.*

- **The tall "sails"** of skin on the backs of the plant eater *Ouranosaurus* and the meat eater *Spinosaurus* may have been for visual display, as well as for (or instead of) temperature control.

- **The large, bony back plates** on stegosaurs may have been used for colorful displays to rivals.

- **The large neck frills** of horned dinosaurs such as *Triceratops* were possibly very colorful and used for display.

- **Recent finds** of dinosaur skin and scales with microscopic ridges and patterns on their surface may show how the scales reflected light, and so what color they would have appeared.

Brains

- **There is a broad link** between the size of an animal's brain compared to the size of its body, and the level of intelligence it shows.

- **Some fossil dinosaur skulls** have preserved the hollow where the brain once was, revealing the approximate size and shape of the brain.

- **In some cases** a lump of rock formed inside a fossil skull, taking on the size and shape of the brain.

- **The tiny brain** of *Stegosaurus* weighed about 3 oz (80 g), while the whole dinosaur weighed up to 2 tons.

▼ Stegosaurus *had the smallest known brain for its body size of any dinosaur—it was about the size of a golfball!*

▼ *Scientists think that it was the small, meat-eating theropods who had the largest brains and therefore, the most intelligence.* Deinonychus, *a pack hunter, was a member of this dinosaur group.*

▼ *A peaceful plant eater,* Stegosaurus *would have had little use for the intelligence of a stealthy hunter like* Troodon.

- **The brain** of *Stegosaurus* was only 1/25,000th of the weight of its whole body (in a human it is 1/50th).

- *Brachiosaurus's* **brain** was perhaps only 1/100,000th of the weight of its whole body.

- **The brain of the small meat eater** *Troodon* was about 1/100th the weight of its whole body.

- **The brain–body size comparison** for most dinosaurs is much the same as the brain–body size for living reptiles.

- **Small and medium-sized meat eaters** such as *Troodon* may have been as "intelligent" as parrots or rats.

- **It was once thought** that *Stegosaurus* had a "second brain" in the base of its tail! Now this lump is thought to have been a nerve junction.

Warm or cold blood?

▶ *In very well-preserved fossils, the detailed microscopic structure inside bones can give clues to whether dinosaurs were warm- or cold-blooded. Also, lizards like this Australian frilled lizard may give us vital clues to dinosaur biology.*

- **If dinosaurs were cold-blooded** and obtained heat only from their surroundings, like reptiles today, they would have been slow or inactive in cold conditions.

- **If dinosaurs were warm-blooded**, like birds and mammals today, they would have been able to stay warm and active in cold conditions.

- **Some time ago** experts believed that all dinosaurs were cold-blooded, but today there is much disagreement.

- **One type of evidence** for warm-bloodedness comes from the detailed structure of the insides of very well-preserved fossil bones.

- **The inside structure** of some fossil dinosaur bones is more like that of warm-blooded creatures than reptiles.

- **Certain small, meat-eating dinosaurs** may have evolved into birds, and since birds are warm-blooded, these dinosaurs may have been, too.

- **In a "snapshot" count** of dinosaur fossils, the number of predators compared to prey is more like that in mammals than in reptiles.

- **Some dinosaurs** were thought to live in herds and raise families, as many birds and mammals do today. In reptiles, such behavior is rare.

- **Most dinosaurs stood upright** on straight legs, a posture common to warm-blooded creatures, but not to other, cold-blooded reptiles.

- **If dinosaurs had been warm-blooded**, they would probably have needed to eat at least ten times more food than if they were cold-blooded, to "burn" food energy and make heat.

◀ *Crocodiles, which were around even in the very earliest dinosaur period (the Triassic) are cold-blooded.*

Nests and eggs

- **There are hundreds of discoveries** of fossil dinosaur eggs and nests, found with the parent dinosaurs.

- **Eggs and nests** are known of the pig-sized plant eater *Protoceratops*, an early kind of horned dinosaur.

- **Many *Protoceratops'*** nests were found in a small area, showing that these dinosaurs bred in colonies.

- ***Protoceratops'* nests** were shallow, bowl-shaped pits about 3 ft (1 m) across, scraped in the dry, sandy earth and surrounded by low walls.

- **At the *Protoceratops* site**, it was discovered that new nests had been made on top of old ones, showing that the colony was used again year after year.

- **The female *Protoceratops*** laid a clutch of 20 or so tough-shelled, sausage-shaped eggs.

- ***Protoceratops'* eggs** were probably covered with earth and incubated by the heat of the sun.

- **Nests and eggs** of the small plant eater *Orodromeus* have been found in Montana.

- **In each nest** about 20 *Orodromeus* eggs were arranged neatly in a spiral, starting with one in the center and working outward.

- ***Protoceratops* arranged** its eggs neatly in its nest, in a circle or spiral shape resembling the spokes of a wheel.

144

▲ *The name* Maiasaura *means "good mother lizard." Paleontologists think that* Maiasaura *cared for its young until they were old enough to look after themselves. It is known that they bred in the same areas each year and may have formed groups to do so, creating a kind of dinosaur nursery!*

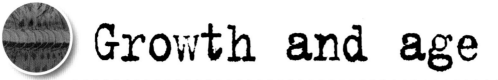

Growth and age

▲ Tyrannosaurus *may have taken between 20 and 50 years to reach adult size. This would depend largely on how much food was available, as in reptiles such as crocodiles today.*

- **No one knows for sure** how fast dinosaurs grew, how long they took to reach full size, or how long they lived.

- **Most estimates** of dinosaur growth rates and ages come from comparisons with today's reptiles.

- **Some reptiles today** continue to grow throughout their lives, although their growth rate slows with age.

- **Dinosaurs** may have grown fast as youngsters and slower as adults, never quite stopping until they died.

- **Estimates for the age of a full-grown meat eater** such as *Tyrannosaurus* range from 20 to more than 50 years.

- **Full-grown, small meat eaters** such as *Compsognathus* may have lived to between three and ten years old.

- **A giant sauropod** probably lived to be about 50 years old, or even over 100 years old.

- **Like many reptiles today**, a dinosaur's growth rate probably depended largely on its food supply.

- **Dinosaurs** probably ate a lot and grew fast when food was plentiful, and slowed down when food was scarce.

- **During its lifetime**, a big sauropod such as *Brachiosaurus* would have increased its weight 2,000 times (compared to 20 times in a human).

Babies

- **As far as we know,** female dinosaurs laid eggs, from which their babies hatched.

- **The time between** eggs being laid and babies hatching out is called the incubation period.

- **Incubation periods** for dinosaur eggs probably varied by weeks or months depending on the temperature, as in today's reptiles.

- **Many fossils** of adult *Maiasaura* (a duckbill dinosaur, or hadrosaur) have been found, together with nests, eggs, and hatchlings (just-hatched babies).

- **Fossils of** *Maiasaura* come mainly from Montana.

◀ *Various clues from fossil evidence show that* Maiasaura *may have brought food back to newly hatched young in the nest. Fossil finds show that leg bones of new hatchlings were not strong enough for them to walk about and feed themselves.*

▲ *The first dinosaur eggs ever discovered were from* Protoceratops. *Paleontologists were able to see that there were tiny holes in the shells to allow air to pass through to the baby dinosaur.*

- **The name** *Maiasaura* means "good mother reptile."
- **The teeth of** *Maiasaura* babies in the nest are slightly worn, showing that they had eaten food.
- **The leg bones and joints** of the *Maiasaura* babies were not quite fully formed, showing that they were not yet able to move about to gather their own food.
- **Evidence** from *Maiasaura* and other nesting sites shows that dinosaurs may have been caring parents, protecting and feeding their young.

149

Coprolites: dino-dung

- **Coprolites** are the fossilized droppings, or dung, of animals from long ago, such as dinosaurs.

- **Dinosaur coprolites** are not soft and smelly—like other fossils, they have become solid rock.

- **Many thousands** of dinosaur coprolites have been found at fossil sites all over the world.

- **Cracking or cutting open** coprolites sometimes reveals what the dinosaur had recently eaten.

- **Coprolites** produced by large meat eaters such as *Tyrannosaurus* contain bone from their prey.

- **The microscopic structure** of the bones found in coprolites shows the age of the prey when it was eaten. Most victims were very young or old, as these were the easiest creatures for a predator to kill.

▲ *Fossilized droppings have been turned to rock, so they are no longer squishy or smelly. Their contents give many clues to dinosaur diets.*

◄ *Fragments of bone have been found in the coprolites of meat-eating dinosaurs such as these* Tyrannosaurus. *Scientists can also find out what plants were growing in a particular period or area by studying the coprolites of herbivorous dinosaurs.*

- **Coprolites produced by small meat eaters** such as *Compsognathus* may contain the hard bits of insects, such as the legs and wing cases of beetles.

- **Huge piles of coprolites** found in Montana, were probably produced by the large plant eater *Maiasaura*.

- *Maiasaura* **coprolites** contain the remains of cones, buds, and the needle-like leaves of conifer trees, showing that these dinosaurs had a tough diet.

...FASCINATING FACT...
One of the largest dinosaur coprolites found was 18 in (44 cm) long and probably produced by *Tyrannosaurus*.

Migration

- **Almost no land reptiles today** go on regular, long-distance journeys, called migrations.

- **Over the past 30 years**, scientists have acquired evidence that some dinosaurs regularly migrated.

- **Evidence for migrating dinosaurs** comes from the positions of the continents at the time. In certain regions, cool winters would have prevented the growth of enough plants for dinosaurs to eat.

- **Fossil evidence suggests** that some plants stopped growing during very hot or dry times, so it is possible that some dinosaurs would have had to migrate to find food.

- **The footprints or tracks** of many dinosaurs traveling in herds is possible evidence that some dinosaurs migrated.

- **Dinosaurs that may have migrated** include *Centrosaurus* and *Pachyrhinosaurus*, sauropods such as *Diplodocus*, and ornithopods such as *Iguanodon* and *Muttaburrasaurus*.

◀ *Few modern reptiles migrate seasonally.*
Centrosaurus, *a dinosaur from the Cretaceous Period, made a migration (indicated here by the arrow) from North America to the sub-Arctic region for the short summer when plant growth was lush.*

▼ *Fossils of* Pachyrhinosaurus *have been found in parts of Alaska that were inside the Arctic Circle at the end of the Cretaceous Period. Since they did not live here permanently, it is reasonable to suppose that they migrated here.*

> **···FASCINATING FACT···**
> Migrating *Centrosaurus* may have walked 60 mi (100 km) a day.

- **One huge fossil site** in Alberta, Canada, contains the fossils of about 1,000 *Pachyrhinosaurus*—perhaps a migrating herd that got caught in a flood.

- **In North America**, huge herds of *Centrosaurus* migrated north for the brief sub-Arctic summer, when plants were abundant, providing plentiful food.

- **In the fall**, *Centrosaurus* herds would have traveled south again to overwinter in the forests.

153

Hibernation

▲ *This is Antarctica as it is today, but throughout the Dinosaur Age, there were no ice caps at the poles at all! However, Australia (where a number of dinosaur fossils have been discovered) was quite close to where Antarctica is now. This means that even with a mild climate, dinosaurs would have faced difficulties in the long winter days.*

- **Dinosaurs may have gone into an inactive state** called hibernation during long periods of cold conditions, as many reptiles do today.

- **Dinosaurs such as the small plant eater** *Leaellynasaura*, found at "Dinosaur Cove," Australia, may have had to hibernate due to the yearly cycle of seasons in the area.

- **Dinosaur Cove, Australia**, was nearer the South Pole when dinosaurs lived there, 120–100 million years ago.

- **The climate** was relatively warm 120–100 million years ago, with no ice at the North or South Poles.

154

- **Dinosaurs at Dinosaur Cove, Australia,** would have had to cope with long hours of darkness during winter, when few plants grew.

- **Australia's Dinosaur Cove dinosaurs** may have hibernated for a few months each year to survive the cool, dark conditions.

- **The eyes and brain shape** of *Leaellynasaura* from Dinosaur Cove, Australia, suggest that this dinosaur had good eyesight.

- *Leaellynasaura* **may have needed** good eyesight to see in the winter darkness, or in the dim forests.

- **Dinosaur fossils** have been found in the Arctic region near the North Pole.

- **Arctic dinosaurs** either hibernated during winter, or migrated south to warmer regions.

▶ Leaellynasaura *may have hibernated through the polar winter, although we cannot be sure.*

...FASCINATING FACT...
Leaellynasaura may have slept through the cold season, perhaps protected in a cave or burrow.

155

Speed

◀ Ornithomimus *was one of the fastest dinosaurs of all! Moving in packs, it would have been able to outrun most predators. The legs were long, slim, and powerful and the stiff tail would have provided balance when running at speed.*

- **The fastest-running dinosaurs** had long, slim, muscular legs and small, lightweight bodies.

- **"Ostrich-dinosaurs"** were probably the speediest dinosaurs, perhaps attaining the same top speed as today's ostrich—40 mph (70 km/h).

- **The main leg muscles** of the ostrich-dinosaur *Struthiomimus* were in its hips and thighs.

- **The hip and leg design** of ostrich-dinosaurs meant that they could swing their limbs to and fro quickly, like those of a modern racehorse.

- **Large, powerful, plant-eating dinosaurs** such as the "duckbill" *Edmontosaurus* may have pounded along on their huge back legs at 25 mph (40 km/h).

- **Plant-eaters** such as *Iguanodon* and *Muttaburrasaurus* may have trotted along at 6–7 mph (10–12 km/h) for many hours.

- **Some experts think** that the great meat eater *Tyrannosaurus* may have been able to run at 30 mph (50 km/h).

- **Other experts think** *Tyrannosaurus* was a relatively slow runner at 20 mph (30 km/h)—almost human sprinting speed.

- **The slowest dinosaurs** were giant sauropods such as *Brachiosaurus*, which probably moved at 2–3 mph (4–6 km/h)—about human walking speed.

- **Today's fastest runner,** the cheetah, would beat any dinosaur with its maximum speed of more than 60 mph (100 km/h).

▶ Brachiosaurus *probably moved around at a walk. Its sheer size would have made speed virtually impossible and its size provided protection from predators.*

157

Herds

- **When the fossils of many individuals** of the same type are found together, there are various possible causes.

- **One reason why** individuals of the same dinosaur type are found preserved together is because their bodies were swept to the same place by a flood.

- **A group of individuals** of the same type may have died in the same place if they had lived there as a group.

- **There is much evidence** that various dinosaur types lived in groups or herds, examples being *Diplodocus, Triceratops,* and *Iguanodon*.

- **Some fossil groups** include dinosaurs of different ages, from newly hatched babies to youngsters and adults.

▶ *Dinosaurs such as the ceratopsian* Centrosaurus *moved about in herds. This may have been partly for protection against predators.*

- **Fossil footprints** suggest some dinosaurs lived in herds.

- **Footprints** of a plant-eating dinosaur were found with the prints of a meat eater to one side of them—perhaps evidence of a hunter pursuing its victim.

- **Sometimes** the footprints of many dinosaurs of the same type are found together, suggesting a herd.

- **Sometimes larger footprints** are found to the sides of smaller ones, possibly indicating that adults guarded their young between them.

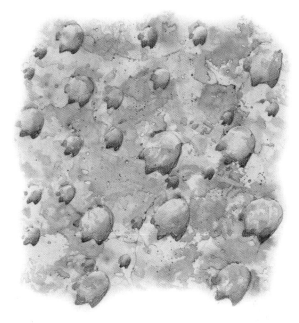

▲ *A mixed-age herd would have left similar footprints of different sizes.*

...**FASCINATING FACT**...
At Peace River Canyon, British Columbia, Canada, some 1,700 footprints were found.

159

Sounds

- **Few reptiles today make sounds,** except for a simple combination of hisses, grunts, and coughs.

- **Fossils suggest that dinosaurs** could have made a variety of sounds in several different ways.

- **The bony, hollow head crests** of duckbills (hadrosaurs) may have been used for making sounds.

- **The head crests of some hadrosaurs** contained tubes called respiratory airways, used for breathing.

- **Air** blown forcefully through a hadrosaur's head crest passages could have made the whole crest vibrate.

- **A hadrosaur's vibrating head crest** may have made a loud sound like a honk, roar, or bellow—similar to an elephant trumpeting with its trunk.

- **Fossil skulls** of some hadrosaurs, such as *Edmontosaurus* and *Kritosaurus*, suggest that there was a loose flap of skin, like a floppy bag, between the nostrils and the eyes.

- ***Kritosaurus*** may have inflated its loose nasal flap of skin like a balloon to make a honking or bellowing sound, as some seals do today.

- **Dinosaurs may have made sounds** to keep in touch with other members of their herd, to frighten away enemies, to intimidate rivals and to impress potential mates at breeding time.

> ...**FASCINATING FACT**...
> By blowing through models of hadrosaur head crests, a wide range of sounds can be made—a bit like those of brass and wind instruments!

Tyrannosaurus
may have been
startled by the
noise of its prey

◀ *In a battle between predator and prey,*
Tyrannosaurus *would have been startled*
or even warned off by the trumpeting of
Parasaurolophus. *The effect of sudden*
noise on the predator may have given
the plant-eating hadrosaur time to
escape. Its noise may have also
summoned members of its herd for
massed defense against the huge
meat eater.

Long, hollow crest
may have resonated
to make a loud call

Powerful rear legs
used for kicking
in self-defense

Tail used for
lashing out

161

North America

▶ Coelophysis *was discovered located in New Mexico, in about 1881. In the late 1940s, another expedition found dozens of skeletons in a mass dinosaur grave.*

- **The majority** of dinosaur fossils have been found in North America.

- **Most dinosaur fossils** in North America come from the dry, rocky "badlands" region, which includes Alberta in Canada, and the U.S. states of Montana, Wyoming, Utah, Colorado, and Arizona.

- **Fossils of the most famous dinosaurs** come from North America, including *Allosaurus, Tyrannosaurus, Diplodocus, Triceratops,* and *Stegosaurus.*

- **Several fossil-rich sites** in North America are now national parks.

- **The U.S. Dinosaur National Monument**, on the border of Utah and Colorado, was established in 1915.

- **The Cleveland-Lloyd Dinosaur Quarry** in Utah contains fossils of stegosaurs, ankylosaurs, sauropods, and meat eaters such as *Allosaurus.*

- **Along the Red Deer River** in Alberta, a large area with thousands of fossils has been designated the Dinosaur Provincial Park.

- **Fossils found in Alberta** include those of the meat eater *Albertosaurus,* armored *Euoplocephalus,* and the duckbill *Lambeosaurus.*

- **The Dinosaur Provincial Park** in Alberta is a United Nations World Heritage Site—the same status as the pyramids of ancient Egypt.

- **A huge, 65-ft (20-m) long plant eater** was named *Alamosaurus* after the famous Battle of the Alamo in Texas in 1836.

▲ *Some of the main dinosaur fossil sites in North America.*

163

South America

- **Many of the most important discoveries** of dinosaur fossils in the last 30 years were made in South America.

- **Dinosaur fossils have been found** from the north to the south of the continent, in the countries of Colombia, Peru, Chile, Brazil, Uruguay, and Argentina.

- **Most dinosaur fossils in South America** have been found on the high grassland, scrub, and semidesert of southern Brazil and Argentina.

- **Some of the earliest known dinosaurs,** such as *Herrerasaurus* and *Eoraptor,* lived more than 225 million years ago in Argentina.

- **Some of the last dinosaurs,** such as the sauropods *Saltasaurus* and *Titanosaurus,* lived in Argentina.

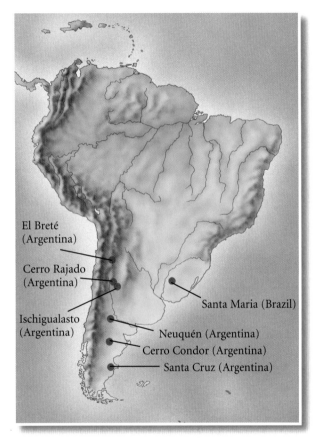

El Breté (Argentina)

Cerro Rajado (Argentina)

Ischigualasto (Argentina)

Santa Maria (Brazil)

Neuquén (Argentina)

Cerro Condor (Argentina)

Santa Cruz (Argentina)

▲ *Dinosaur fossils found in South America since the 1970s have revealed unique kinds of dinosaur. These include the biggest predatory dinosaurs, some of the earliest members of the dinosaur group, and possibly the largest of all dinosaurs.*

◄ *At the dawn of the dinosaur age, meat eaters such as* Herrerasaurus *were about in South America—some of the last dinosaurs lived there too.*

- **Fossils of the meat-eating predator** *Piatnitzkyosaurus* come from Cerro Condo in southern Argentina.

- *Piatnitzkyosaurus* **was similar** to the great predator *Allosaurus* of North America, but at 13–16 ft (4–5 m) long was less than half its size.

- **Like many dinosaurs in Argentina**, *Piatnitzkyosaurus* lived during the Middle Jurassic Period.

- **Remains of about ten huge** *Patagosaurus* sauropods were found in the fossil-rich region of Chubut, Argentina, from 1977.

. . .FASCINATING FACT. . .
Some of the biggest of all dinosaurs, including the largest meat eater *Giganotosaurus* and the vast sauropod *Argentinosaurus* come from Argentina.

Europe

- **The first dinosaur fossils** ever discovered and given official names were found in England.

- **One of the first almost complete dinosaur skeletons** found was that of the big plant eater *Iguanodon*, in 1871, in southern England.

- **Some of the most numerous early fossils found** were those of *Iguanodon*, discovered in a coal mine in the Belgian village of Bernissart in 1878.

- **About 155–150 million years ago,** Solnhofen in southern Germany was a mosaic of lush islands and shallow lagoons—ideal for many kinds of life.

▲ *During the Jurassic Period, 248–208 million years ago, much of Europe would have looked like this. There was a much warmer, damper, more tropical climate, where ferns, ginkgoes, horsetails, and cycads flourished alongside forests of conifers and tree ferns.*

- **In sandstone** in the Solnhofen region of Germany, fossils of amazing detail preserved the tiny *Compsognathus* and the first known bird, *Archaeopteryx*.

- **Fossils of tiny *Compsognathus*** were found near Nice in southern France.

- **Many fossils** of the plant-eating prosauropod *Plateosaurus* were recovered from Trossingen, Germany, in 1911–1912, 1921–1923, and 1932.

- **Some of the largest fossil dinosaur eggs**, measuring 12 in (30 cm) long (five times longer than a hen's egg), were thought to have been laid by the sauropod *Hypselosaurus* near Aix-en-Provence in southern France.

- **The Isle of Wight** off southern England has provided so many dinosaur fossils that it is sometimes known as "Dinosaur Island."

- **Fossils of** *Hypsilophodon* have been found in eastern Spain, and those of *Camptosaurus* on the coast of Portugal.

Stonesfield (England)
Elgin (Scotland)
Ockley (England)
Halberstadt (Germany)
Bernissart (Belgium)
Kelheim (Germany)
Charmouth (England)
Friek (Switzerland)
Solnhofen (Germany)
Swanage (England)
Isle of Wight (England)
Nice (France)
Trossingham (Germany)
Aix-en-Provence (France)
Torres Vedras (Portugal)
Morella (Spain)

▲ *Dinosaur fossils are often found in Europe.*

167

Africa

▼ Jobaria *(Sahara region) and*
Janenschia *(Malawi and Tanzania)*
are two giant sauropod dinosaurs
recently discovered in Africa.

- **The first major discoveries** of dinosaur fossils in Africa were made from 1907, at Tendaguru in present-day Tanzania, east Africa.

- **Discoveries at Tendaguru** in east Africa included the giant sauropod *Brachiosaurus*, the smaller *Dicraeosaurus*, and the stegosaurlike Kentrosaurus.

- **Remains** of the massive sauropod *Cetiosaurus* were uncovered in Morocco, north Africa.

- *Camarasaurus*, **a 20-ton plant eater**, is known from fossils found in Niger, as well as from European and North American fossils.

- **Fossils** of the huge, sail-backed meat eater *Spinosaurus* come from Morocco and Egypt.

- **The sail-backed plant eater** *Ouranosaurus* is known from remains found in Niger.

- **Many sauropod fossils** were uncovered at sites in Zimbabwe, including *Barosaurus* and *Vulcanodon*.

- **Remains** of the medium-sized plant-eating prosauropod *Massospondylus* were extracted from several sites in southern Africa.

- **Fossils** thought to belong to the small prosauropod *Anchisaurus* were found in southern Africa, the only site for this dinosaur outside North America.

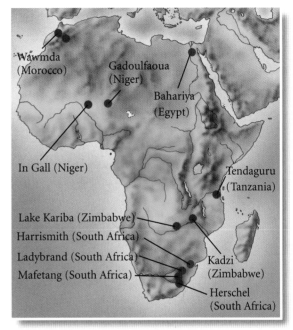

▲ *In Africa, as elsewhere, fossils are easier to find in places with bare, rocky soils.*

- **During the 1908–1912 fossil-hunting expedition** to Tendaguru, more than 275 tons of fossil bones and rocks were carried by people for 40 mi (65 km) to the nearest port, for transport to Germany.

Gobi Desert

- **The Gobi** covers much of southern Mongolia and parts of northern China. During the Age of Dinosaurs, it was a land of scrub and scattered trees.

- **The first fossil-hunting expeditions** to the Gobi Desert took place in 1922–1925, organized by the American Museum of Natural History.

- **The 1922–1925 Gobi expeditions** set out to look for fossils of very early humans, but instead found some amazing dinosaur remains.

- **The first fossil dinosaur eggs** were found by the 1922–1925 expeditions.

- *Velociraptor, Avimimus,* and *Pinacosaurus* were discovered in the Gobi.

- **Russian fossil-hunting trips** into the Gobi Desert in 1946 and 1948–1949 discovered new types of armored dinosaurs, duck-billed dinosaurs, and the huge meat eater *Tarbosaurus*.

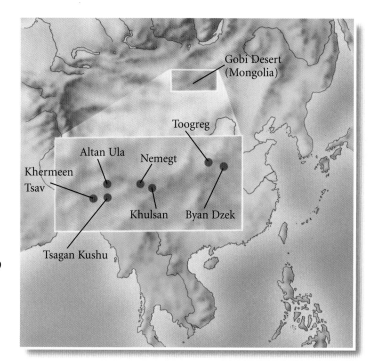

Gobi Desert (Mongolia)

Toogreg

Altan Ula

Nemegt

Khermeen Tsav

Khulsan

Byan Dzek

Tsagan Kushu

▲ *The Gobi's fossil sites are far from any towns.*

▲ *The temperature in the Gobi Desert can be severe, with fluctuations of 145°F (80°C) between winter and summer. The climate is harsh and dry, but many interesting fossil finds have been made there.*

- **More expeditions to the Gobi** in the 1960s–1970s, especially to the fossil-rich area of the Nemegt Basin, found the giant sauropod *Opisthocoelicaudia* and the "helmet-headed" *Prenocephale*.

- **Other dinosaurs** found in the Gobi include the ostrich-dinosaur *Gallimimus* and the strong-beaked "egg thief" *Oviraptor*.

- **The Gobi Desert** can be –40°F (–40°C) in winter and 104°F (40°C) in summer.

- **Despite the harsh conditions**, the Gobi Desert is one of the most exciting areas in the world for finding dinosaur fossils.

Asia

- **Hundreds of kinds of dinosaurs** have been discovered on the continent of Asia.

- **In Asia**, most of the dinosaur fossils that have been found so far were located in the Gobi Desert, in Central Asia, and in present-day China. Some were also found in present-day India.

- **Remains of the huge plant-eating sauropod** *Titanosaurus* were uncovered near Umrer, in central India.

- *Titanosaurus* was about 40 ft (12 m) long and weighed 5–10 tons.

- *Titanosaurus* **lived about 70 million years ago**, and was very similar in shape to its close cousin of the same time, *Saltasaurus*, from South America.

▼ Tuojiangosaurus *is sometimes portrayed as having its legs bent out to the sides, like a lizard, but paleontologists now think that they were much straighter, like those of other dinosaurs. Theories about dinosaurs are constantly being updated and revised—that's what makes them so exciting!*

- **Fossils** of the sauropod *Barapasaurus* were found in India. They date from the Early Jurassic Period, about 180 million years ago.

- ***Barapasaurus*** was 60 ft (18 m) long and probably weighed more than 20 tons.

- **Fossils** of the dinosaur *Dravidosaurus*, from the stegosaur group, were found near Tiruchirapalli in southern India.

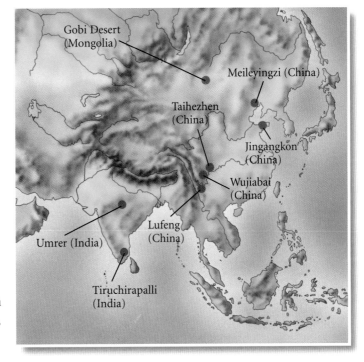

▲ *Dinosaur fossil finds span this vast continent.*

- ***Dravidosaurus*** was about 10 ft (3 m) in total length. It lived much later than other stegosaurs, in the Late Cretaceous Period about 70 million years ago.

- ***Dravidosaurus* had bony plates** sticking up from its back, like *Stegosaurus*.

173

China

- **For centuries**, dinosaur fossils in China were identified as belonging to folklore creatures such as dragons.

- **The first dinosaur fossils** studied scientifically in China were uncovered in the 1930s.

- **Because of China's political isolation in the past**, many dinosaur fossils found there remained unknown to scientists in other countries.

- **From the 1980s**, dinosaur discoveries in almost every province of China have amazed scientists from around the globe.

▼ Caudipteryx *was an unusual dinosaur that lived in what is now China. Like all scaly or feathery reconstructions, the colors of this bird-reptile are the result of intelligent guesswork.*

···**FASCINATING FACT**···
Of all the world's countries, probably only the U.S.A. has more fossil dinosaurs than China.

- **A few exciting dinosaur finds** in China have been fakes, such as part of a bird skeleton that was joined to the part-skeleton of a dinosaur along a natural-looking crack in the rock.

- **Some better-known Chinese finds** of dinosaurs include *Mamenchisaurus, Psittacosaurus, Tuojiangosaurus,* and *Avimimus.*

- **Remains of the prosauropod** *Lufengosaurus* were uncovered in China's southern province of Yunnan, in 1941.

- **China's** *Lufengosaurus* lived during the Early Jurassic Period, and measured about 20–23 ft (6–7 m) long.

- **Many recently found fossils** in China are of feathered dinosaurs.

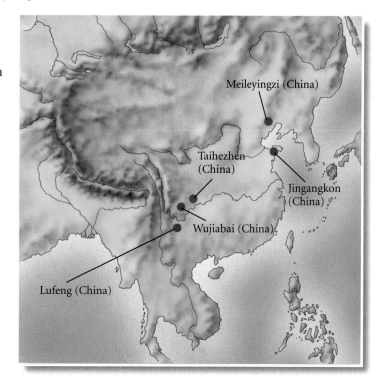

▲ *Recent fossil finds in China are causing scientists to change many long-held ideas.*

Australia

▶ *Many exciting fossils have been found in Australia over the past 40 years, with most unique to this region, the smallest of all the continents.*

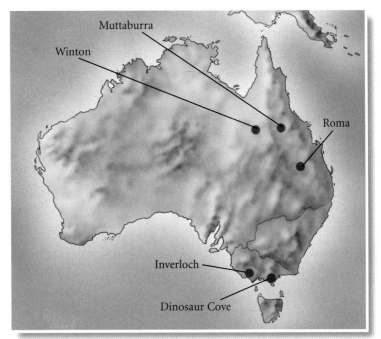

Muttaburra

Winton

Roma

Inverloch

Dinosaur Cove

- **In the past 40 years**, some of the most exciting discoveries of dinosaur fossils have come from Australia.

- **Remains of the large plant eater** *Muttaburrasaurus* were found near Muttaburra, Queensland.

- *Muttaburrasaurus* was about 23 ft (7 m) long and similar in some ways to the well-known plant eater *Iguanodon*.

- **Fossils of** *Rhoetosaurus*, a giant plant eater, were found in 1924 in southern Queensland.

- **The sauropod *Rhoetosaurus*** was 57 ft (17 m) long and lived 170 million years ago.

- **Near Winton, Queensland**, more than 3,300 footprints show where about 130 dinosaurs once passed by.

> ...**FASCINATING FACT**...
> Dinosaur Cove is difficult to reach, and many of the fossils are in hard rocks in the middle of sheer cliffs with pounding waves far beneath.

- **One of the major new fossil sites** in Australia is "Dinosaur Cove," on the coast near Melbourne, Victoria.

- **Fossil-rich rocks** at "Dinosaur Cove" are part of the Otway-Strzelecki mountain ranges, and are 120–100 million years old.

- **Remains found at "Dinosaur Cove"** include *Leaellynasaura* and a smaller version of the huge meat eater *Allosaurus*.

◄ Muttaburasaurus *lived 110 million years ago in what is now New South Wales, Australia. It was bipedal (it walked on two legs), a cousin of* Iguanodon, *and weighed about 4 tons.*

177

Age of Dinosaurs

- **The Age of Dinosaurs** corresponds to the time period that geologists call the Mesozoic Era, from about 248–65 million years ago.

- **The Mesozoic Era** is divided into three shorter time spans—the Triassic, Jurassic and Cretaceous Periods.

- **During the Triassic Period,** 248–208 million years ago, the dinosaurs began to evolve.

- **During the Jurassic Period**—about 208–144 million years ago—the dinosaurs reached their greatest size.

- **The Cretaceous Period** is when dinosaurs were at their most varied—about 144–65 million years ago.

- **In the Triassic Period**, all the continents were joined together in one supercontinent—Pangaea.

- **In the Jurassic Period**, the supercontinent of Pangaea separated into two huge land masses—Laurasia in the north and Gondwanaland in the south.

Pangaea

Gondwanaland

Laurasia

▼ *The continents as they are today.*

▶ *200 million years ago, Pangaea split into two huge continents called Laurasia and Gondwanaland. Even today the continents are still moving.*

YEARS AGO (MILLIONS)	ERA	PERIOD	
80		CRETACEOUS	
100		CRETACEOUS	
120		CRETACEOUS	
140	MESOZOIC	CRETACEOUS	AGE OF REPTILES
160	MESOZOIC	JURASSIC	AGE OF REPTILES
180	MESOZOIC	JURASSIC	AGE OF REPTILES
200		JURASSIC	
220		TRIASSIC	

◀ *Dinosaurs ruled the land for 160 million years— longer than any other animal group.*

- **In the Cretaceous Period**, Laurasia and Gondwanaland split, and the continents as we know them began to form.

- **In the Mesozoic Era,** the major land-masses gradually moved across the globe in a process known as "continental drift."

- **The joining and separating** of the continents affected which kinds of dinosaurs lived where. During the Triassic Period, the earliest mammals and the first dinosaurs appeared.

179

Names: 1

- **Every dinosaur has a scientific name**, usually made up from Latin or Greek, and written in italics.

- **Many dinosaur names** end in -saurus, which some say means "reptile" and others say means "lizard"—even though dinosaurs were not lizards.

- **Dinosaur names** often refer to a feature that no other dinosaur had. *Baryonyx*, for example, means "heavy claw," a name taken from the massive claw on its thumb.

- **The medium-sized meat eater** *Herrerasaurus* from Argentina was named after Victorino Herrera, the farmer who first noticed its fossils.

- **Many dinosaur names are real tongue twisters**, such as *Opisthocoelicaudia*, pronounced "owe-pis-thowe-see-lee-cord-ee-ah."

- ***Opisthocoelicaudia*** means "posterior tail cavity," and refers to the joints between the backbones in the tail.

▼ *The naming of* Troodon *was originally based on the finding of a single curved, serrated "wounding" tooth.*

▶ *Some well-known predators from the Age of Dinosaurs!*

180

- **Some dinosaurs** were named after the place where their fossils were found. Minmi was located near Minmi Crossing in Queensland, Australia.

> ....FASCINATING FACT....
> *Triceratops*, or "three-horned face," is one of the best-known dinosaur scientific names.

- **Some dinosaur groups** are named after the first-discovered or major one of its kind, such as the tyrannosaurs or stegosaurs.

- **The fast-running ostrich-dinosaurs' name,** ornithomimosaurs, means "bird-mimic reptiles."

MEAT EATERS:

Troodon *Meaning:* wounding tooth *Pronounced:* TROH-oh-don/Late Cretaceous	**Tyrannosaurus** *Meaning:* tyrant lizard *Pronounced:* tie-RAN-oh-sore-us/Late Cretaceous	**Ornitholestes** *Meaning:* bird robber *Pronounced:* Or-nith-oh- LES –teez/Late Jurassic
Oviraptor *Meaning:* egg thief *Pronounced:* OH-vee-RAP-tor/Late Cretaceous	**Dilophosaurus** *Meaning:* two-ridged lizard *Pronounced:* die-LOAF-oh-sore-us/Early Jurassic	**Coelurus** *Meaning:* hollow tail *Pronounced:* seel-YEW-rus/Late Jurassic
Baryonyx *Meaning:* heavy claw *Pronounced:* bah-ree-ON-icks/Late Jurassic	**Coelophysis** *Meaning:* hollow form *Pronounced:* seel-OH-fie-sis/Late Triassic	**Tarbosaurus** *Meaning:* alarming lizard *Pronounced:* TAR-bow-SORE-us/Late Cretaceous
Deinonychus *Meaning:* terrible claw *Pronounced:* die-NON-i-kuss/Early Cretaceous	**Velociraptor** *Meaning:* quick plunderer *Pronounced:* vel-OSS-ee-rap-tor/Late Cretaceous	**Struthiomimus** *Meaning:* ostrich mimic *Pronounced:* STRUTH-ee-oh-MEEM-us/Late Cretaceous

Names: 2

- **More than 100 kinds of dinosaurs** have been named after the people who first discovered their fossils, dug them up, or reconstructed the dinosaur.

- **The very large duckbill (hadrosaur)** *Lambeosaurus* was named after Canadian fossil expert Lawrence Lambe.

- **Lawrence Lambe** worked mainly during the early 1900s, and named one of his finds *Stephanosaurus*.

- **In the 1920s,** *Stephanosaurus* was re-studied and renamed, along with *Didanodon*, as *Lambeosaurus*, in honor of Lambe's great work.

- **The full name** of the "heavy-claw" meat eater *Baryonyx* is *Baryonyx walkeri*, after Bill Walker, the discoverer of its massive claw.

- **Part-time fossil hunter** Bill Walker found the claw of *Baryonyx* in a clay pit quarry in Surrey, England.

▶ *The name* Orodromeus *means "mountain runner," from its fossil site in the rocky uplands of Montana. It had a slim, light, fast-moving build and was only 6 ft (2 m) in total length.*

...**FASCINATING FACT**...
Australian *Leaellynasaura* was named after Lea Ellyn, the daughter of its discoverers.

HERBIVORES:

Plateosaurus *Meaning:* flat lizard *Pronounced:* plat-ee-oh-sore-us/Late Triassic	**Iguanodon** *Meaning:* iguana tooth *Pronounced:* ig-WHA-noh-don/Early Cretaceous	**Segnosaurus** *Meaning:* slow lizard *Pronounced:* SEG-no-SORE-us/Late Cretaceous
Brachiosaurus *Meaning:* arm lizard *Pronounced:* BRAK-ee-oh-sore-us/Late Jurassic	**Psittacosaurus** *Meaning:* parrot lizard *Pronounced:* SIT-ak-oh-sore-us/Early Cretaceous	**Seismosaurus** *Meaning:* earth-shaking lizard *Pronounced:* SIZE-moh-SORE-us/Late Jurassic
Heterodontosaurus *Meaning:* different-teeth lizard *Pronounced:* HET-er-oh-DON'T-oh-sore-us/Early Jurassic	**Ankylosaurus** *Meaning:* stiff lizard *Pronounced:* an-KIE-loh-sore-us/Late Cretaceous	**Orodromeus** *Meaning:* mountain runner *Pronounced:* or-oh-DROM-ee-us/Late Cretaceous
Camarasaurus *Meaning:* chambered lizard *Pronounced:* KAM-ar-a-sore-us/Late Jurassic	**Pachycephalosaurus** *Meaning:* thick-headed lizard *Pronounced:* pack-i-KEF-al-oh-sore-russ/Late Cretaceous	**Saltasaurus** *Meaning:* Salta reptile *Pronounced:* Salt-AH-sore-us/Late Cretaceous

▲ *These are just a few of the plant-eating dinosaurs that existed during the Age of Dinosaurs.*

- **Some dinosaur names** are quite technical, such as *Diplodocus*, which means "double beam"—it was named for its tail bones, which have two long projections like a pair of skis.

- **The 13-ft (4-m) long plant eater** *Othnielia*, related to *Hypsilophodon*, was named after the American fossil hunter Othniel Charles Marsh.

- *Parksosaurus*, an 8-ft (2.5-m) long plant eater related to *Hypsilophodon*, was named in honor of Canadian dinosaur expert William Parks.

183

Archosaurs

▲ *The archosaur* Ornithosuchus *outwardly resembled some of the Jurassic and Cretaceous meat eaters. However, it was probably not a dinosaur but a close cousin.*

- **Archosaurs** were a very large group of reptiles that included the dinosaurs as one of their subgroups.

- **Other archosaur subgroups** included thecodonts, flying reptiles called pterosaurs, and crocodiles.

- **The thecodonts** included a smaller reptile group, the ornithosuchians—possibly the dinosaurs' ancestors.

- **One of the most dinosaur-like of the archosaurs** was the thecodont *Ornithosuchus.*

▶ Rhamphorhynchus *measured about 3 ft (1 m) across its wingtips. Its fossils date from the same time, the Late Jurassic Period, and the same area, Southern Germany, as the fossils of the earliest known bird,* Archaeopteryx.

- **The 13-ft (4-m) long** *Ornithosuchus* stood almost upright.

- ***Ornithosuchus* fossils** were found in Scotland.

- **Sharp-toothed** *Ornithosuchus* was probably a powerful predator.

- **Features** in *Ornithosuchus*'s backbone, hips, and feet indicate that it was almost certainly not a dinosaur.

- **The archosaur** *Longisquama* was a lizard-like reptile only 6 in (15 cm) long, with tall scales forming a V-shaped row along its back.

- **Archosaur means "ruling reptile,"** and archosaurs did indeed rule the land, swamps and skies for over 170 million years.

Cousins: land

- **Land animals** during the Age of Dinosaurs included insects, spiders, other reptiles, birds, and mammals.

- **Dinosaurs** had many large, fierce, reptile enemies.

- **One of the biggest** non-dinosaur land reptiles was *Deinosuchus* (or *Phobosuchus*), a type of crocodile.

- *Deinosuchus* lived in the Late Cretaceous Period, in present-day Texas.

- **The fossil skull** of *Deinosuchus* measures about 6 ft (2 m) long, much bigger than any crocodile of today.

- **The first mammals** appeared on Earth at about the same time as the early dinosaurs.

▲ Megazostrodon *was one of the earliest mammals, living alongside the first dinosaurs about 200 million years ago. It was a tiny, furry creature that looked a little bit like a rat.*

▼ Chasmatosaurus (Proterosuchus) *was a very early member of the thecodont group. It spent the majority of its time in the water and looked similar to a modern crocodile.*

- **Various kinds of mammals** survived all through the Age of Dinosaurs, although none grew larger than a pet cat.

- **One of the first mammals** known from fossils is *Megazostrodon*, which resembled a shrew of today.

- ***Megazostrodon* was just 5 in (12 cm) long** and its fossils, from 220–210 million years ago, come from southern Africa.

- **If *Deinosuchus's* body** was in proportion to its skull, it would have been 50 ft (15 m) long!

Cousins: sea

▲ *Ichthyosaurs were a group of sea-dwelling, meat-eating reptiles that thrived alongside the dinosaurs. Like the dinosaurs, they all became extinct at the end of the Cretaceous Period.*

- **Placodont reptiles** lived mainly during the Triassic Period. They were shaped like large salamanders or turtles, and probably ate shellfish.

- **The placodont** *Placodus* was about 6 ft (2 m) long and looked like a large, scaly newt.

- **The nothosaurs** were fish-eating reptiles of the Triassic Period. They had small heads, long necks and tails, and four flipper-shaped limbs.

- **Fossils** of the 10 ft (3 m) long nothosaur *Nothosaurus* have been found across Europe, Asia, and Africa.

- **The dolphin-like ichthyosaur reptiles** had back fins, two-lobed tails, and flipper-shaped limbs.

- **Many kinds of ichthyosaurs** thrived in the seas during the Triassic and Jurassic Periods, although they had faded away by the middle of the Cretaceous Period.

- **One of the biggest ichthyosaurs** was *Shonisaurus*, which measured up to 50 ft (15 m) long.

- **The plesiosaurs** were fish-eating reptiles of the Mesozoic Era, with small heads, plump bodies, four flipper-shaped limbs, and short, tapering tails.

- **The plesiosaur** *Elasmosaurus* was up to 47 ft (14 m) long, with more than half of this length being its extraordinarily long, snakelike neck.

▼ *Very finely preserved fossils of* Nothosaurus *reveal the outline of the skin between the toes, showing they were webbed. This long, flexible sea reptile probably hunted fish, squid, and other prey, much as dolphins and seals do today.*

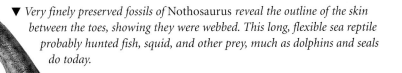

.....FASCINATING FACT.....
One of the biggest meat eaters ever was the short-necked plesiosaur *Liopleurodon*, at 66 ft (20 m) long and 50 tons in weight.

189

Cousins: air

▲ *With a wingspan of 40 ft (12 m),* Quetzalcoatlus *holds the record for being the largest flying creature ever! Like other pterosaurs, it had a long slim beak for fishing, but it may also have fed on carrion (carcasses of dead animals).*

- **Many flying creatures** lived during the Age of Dinosaurs, especially insects such as flies and dragonflies, and also birds.

- **The main flying reptiles** during the Age of Dinosaurs were the pterosaurs, or "winged reptiles."

- **Hundreds of different kinds** of pterosaurs came and went through almost the entire Age of Dinosaurs, about 220–65 million years ago.

- **The arms of a pterosaur** resembled wings—a light, thin, stretchy wing membrane was held out mainly by the finger bones, especially the fourth finger.

◀ Rhamphorhynchoid *was a fearsome-looking creature with a long jaw lined with sharp forward-pointing teeth. Its long tail is typical of the rhamphorhychoid group.*

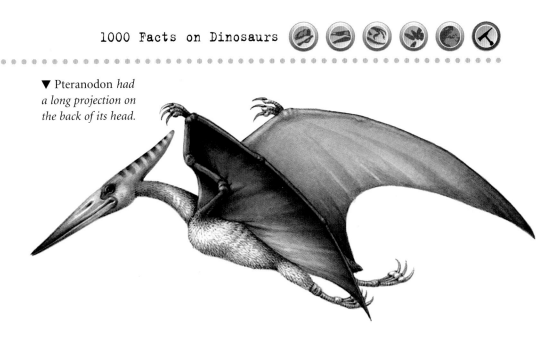

▼ Pteranodon *had a long projection on the back of its head.*

- **Pterosaurs** are sometimes called pterodactyls, but *Pterodactylus* was just one kind of pterosaur.

- *Pterodactylus* **had a wingspan** of 3–6 ft (1–2 m). It lived 150–140 million years ago in southern Germany.

- **Some pterosaurs**, such as *Pterodactylus*, had very short tails, or no tail at all.

- **The pterosaur** *Rhamphorhynchus* had a long, trailing tail with a widened, paddle-shaped end.

- **Fossils** suggest that some pterosaurs, such as Sordes, had fur, and may have been warm-blooded, agile fliers rather than slow, clumsy gliders.

- **The biggest pterosaur**, and the largest flying animal ever, was *Quetzalcoatlus*. Its "beak" was longer than the height of an adult human, and its wingspan was almost 40 ft (12 m)!

191

Extinction

▶ *We can only guess at the havoc when a massive meteorite hit Earth, 65 million years ago. Whether this was the main cause of the mass extinction, or the "last straw" following other problems, is not clear. What we do know is that all dinosaurs perished along with ichthyosaurs, plesiosaurs (sea-dwelling beasts) and pterosaurs (flying reptiles). Why did these species die out when others, such as the mammals, survived?*

● **All dinosaurs on Earth** had died out, or become extinct, by 65 million years ago.

● **Many other reptiles**, such as pterosaurs and plesiosaurs, and many other animals and plants disappeared with the dinosaurs, in a "mass extinction."

● **A possible cause** of the mass extinction was a new kind of disease that swept across the land and seas.

> **· · · FASCINATING FACT · · ·**
> Scientists found a huge crater—the Chixulub Crater—under seabed mud off the coast of Yucatan, Mexico. This could be where a giant meteorite hit Earth 65 million years ago.

- **The mass extinction** of the dinosaurs and other animals may have been due to a series of huge volcanic eruptions that filled the air with poisonous fumes.

- **Climate change** is another possible cause of the mass extinction—perhaps a period of global warming that lasted for a few hundred years, or even longer.

- **One theory** for the mass extinction is that a giant lump of rock from space— a meteorite—hit Earth.

- **A giant meteorite** 6 mi (10 km) across smashing into Earth would have set off earthquakes and volcanoes, and thrown up vast amounts of dust to darken the skies.

▲ *A massive meteorite may have killed off the dinosaurs.*

- **Skies darkened by dust for one year or more** would mean the death of many plants, and so the death of plant-eating animals, and consequently the meat eaters.

- **One great puzzle** about the disappearance of the dinosaurs is why similar reptiles, such as crocodiles, lizards, and turtles, survived.

After dinosaurs

- **The Age of Dinosaurs** came to a fairly sudden end 65 million years ago. We know this from rocks and fossils, which changed dramatically at that time.

- **The Cretaceous Period** ended 65 million years ago.

- **There are no dinosaur fossils** after 65 million years ago.

- **Many animal groups**, including fish, crocodiles, turtles, lizards, birds, and mammals, survived the extinction that took place 65 million years ago.

- **Birds and mammals** in particular underwent rapid changes after the dinosaurs disappeared.

- **Within ten million years** of the dinosaurs' demise, bats, primates, armadillos, hoofed mammals, and rodents had all appeared.

- **The land mammal** that came closest to rivalling the great size of the dinosaurs was *Indricotherium*, also known as *Baluchitherium*.

- *Indricotherium* was 27 ft (8 m) long, 16 ft (5 m) tall, and weighed perhaps 27 tons.

- *Indricotherium* was less than half the size of the biggest dinosaurs.

▲ *The outsized dinosaurs were followed by outsized mammals, such as* Indricotherium *(far right), three times bigger than elephants of today.*

...FASCINATING FACT...
Some people believe that dinosaurs may still be alive today, deep in tropical forests or in remote valleys—but no firm evidence exists.

195

Fossil formation

- **Most of the information** we know, or guess, about dinosaurs comes from fossils.

- **Fossils are the remains of once-living things** that have been preserved in rocks and turned to stone, usually over millions of years.

- **Not just dinosaurs**, but many kinds of living things from prehistoric times have left fossils, including mammals, birds, lizards, fish, insects, and plants such as ferns and trees.

- **The flesh, guts, and other soft parts** of a dead dinosaur's body were probably eaten by scavengers, or rotted away, and so rarely formed fossils.

- **Fossils usually formed** when a dinosaur's remains were quickly covered by sediments such as sand, silt, or mud, especially along the banks of a river or lake, or on the seashore.

- **The sand or other sediment** around a creature or plant's remains was gradually buried deeper by more sediment, squeezed under pressure, and cemented together into a solid mass of rock.

- **As the sediment turned to rock**, so did the plant or animal remains encased within it.

- **Information about dinosaurs** comes not only from fossils, but also from "trace" fossils. These were not actual parts of their bodies, but other items or signs of their presence.

- **These include** egg shells, footprints, marks made by claws and teeth, and coprolites—fossilized dinosaur droppings.

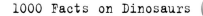 
▶ *Fossil formation is a very long process, and extremely prone to chance and luck. Only a tiny fraction of animals that ever lived, have left remains preserved by this process. Because of the way fossils formed, animals that died in water or along banks and shores were most likely to be fossilized.*

1. Animal died and its soft parts were scavenged or rotted away

2. Sand, mud, or other sediments covered the hard parts such as the shell, teeth, and bones

4. Erosion (wearing away) of upper rock layers expose the fossils, which are now solid stone

3. More layers built up above, as the minerals in the bones, shell and other hard parts turn to rock

197

Dinosaur fossil hunters

- **Many dinosaurs** were found in the United States in the 1870s–1890s by Othniel Charles Marsh and Edward Drinker Cope.

- **Marsh and Cope** were great rivals, each one trying to find bigger, better, and more dinosaur fossils than the other.

- **The rivalry between Marsh and Cope** extended to bribing people to smash each other's fossils with hammers, planting fake fossils, and damaging food, water, and other supplies at each other's camps in the west.

- **Cope and Marsh found and described** about 130 new kinds of dinosaurs between 1877 and 1897.

- **Joseph Tyrrell** discovered fossils of *Albertosaurus* in 1884, in what became a very famous dinosaur region, the Red Deer River area of Alberta, Canada.

- **Lawrence Lambe** found and described many North American dinosaur fossils, such as *Centrosaurus* in 1904.

- **German fossil experts** Werner Janensch and Edwin Hennig led expeditions to east Africa in 1908–1912, and discovered *Brachiosaurus* and *Kentrosaurus*.

- **From 1933** Yang Zhong-jiang (also called C.C. Young) led many fossil-hunting trips in various parts of China.

- **José Bonaparte** from Argentina has found many fossils in that region, including *Carnotaurus* in 1985.

▲ *Othniel Charles Marsh (left) and Edward Drinker Cope (right) had a rivalry between them that came to be known as the "Bone Wars." Allegedly, this began when Marsh pointed out a mistake that Cope had made with the reconstruction of a plesiosaur skeleton. Cope never forgave him, but the rift led to the discovery of almost 140 new dinosaur species!*

. . . **FASCINATING FACT** . . .
One of the first great U.S. fossil hunters was
Joseph Leidy, who found *Troodon* in 1856.

Reconstructions

- **No complete fossilized dinosaur**, with all its skin, muscles, guts, and other soft parts, has yet been found.

- **Most dinosaurs are reconstructed** from the fossil remains of their hard parts—chiefly teeth, bones, horns, and claws.

- **The vast majority of dinosaurs** are known from only a few fossil parts, such as several fragments of bones.

- **Fossil parts** of other, similar dinosaurs are often used in reconstructions to "fill in" missing bones, teeth, and even missing heads, limbs, or tails.

- **Soft body parts** from modern reptiles such as lizards are used as a guide for the reconstruction of a dinosaur's muscles and guts, which are added to the fossils.

- **On rare occasions**, remains are found of a dinosaur body that dried out rapidly so that quite a few parts were preserved as mummified fossils.

- **One of the best-known**, part-mummified dinosaur fossils is "Sue," a specimen of *Tyrannosaurus* found in 1990 in South Dakota.

- **"Sue" is the biggest** and most complete preserved *Tyrannosaurus* ever found.

- **"Sue" was a female** *Tyrannosaurus*. It was named after its discoverer, fossil hunter Susan Hendrickson of the Black Hills Institute of Geological Research.

▲ *Fossils must be handled very carefully to avoid any damage: remember, they are millions of years old! In the paleontology laboratory, they are cleaned with special equipment.*

▲ *After cleaning, the fossils are laid out to show the dinosaur skeleton. Scientists then reconstruct body parts, such as skin and internal organs.*

▲ *Finally, the rebuilt skeleton is displayed
in a museum.*

Mysteries

▲ *When* Troodon*'s tooth was first discovered, it was thought to belong to a carnivorous lizard such as this monitor lizard. However, scientists later discovered that it was from the most intelligent dinosaur ever!*

- **Some dinosaurs have been named** on very scant evidence, such as a single bit of fossil bone, or just one tooth or claw.

- **The small meat eater** *Troodon* was named in 1856 on the evidence of a single tooth.

- **The first tooth** *Troodon* **tooth** was found in the Judith River region of Montana.

- **At first,** the tooth of *Troodon* was thought to have come from a lizard such as a monitor lizard.

- **In the early 1900s,** more *Troodon*-like teeth were found in Alberta and Wyoming, and were believed to have come from a pachycephalosaur or "bone-head" dinosaur.

- **In the 1980s**, a fuller picture of *Troodon* was built up by putting its teeth together with other fossils, including bones.

- **Only parts of the hands and arms** of *Deinocheirus* have been found. They were discovered in Mongolia, Central Asia, in the 1970s.

- **It is possible** that *Deinocheirus* was a gigantic ostrich-dinosaur, perhaps as tall as a giraffe, at 16–20 ft (5–6 m).

- ***Therizinosaurus*, or "scythe reptile,"** was a huge dinosaur known only from a few parts of its limbs. It lived in the Late Cretaceous Period in Mongolia, Central Asia.

- **A mysterious fossil claw** was found, thought possibly to belong to *Therizinosaurus*, and measuring about 3 ft (1 m) around its outer curve.

▶ Deinocheirus, *known only from a few fossil pieces of arm and hand, could have been an ostrich-dinosaur like this—but as tall as a giraffe!*

Inventing the "dinosaur"

- **When fossils of dinosaurs were first studied** by scientists in the 1820s, they were thought to be from huge lizards, rhinoceroses, or even whales.

- **The first dinosaur** to be given an official name was *Megalosaurus*, by English clergyman William Buckland in 1824.

- **Fossils of dinosaurs** were found and studied in 1822 by Gideon Mantell, a country doctor in Sussex, southern England.

- **In 1825,** Englishman Gideon Mantell named his creature *Iguanodon*, because its fossil teeth were very similar in shape to, but larger than, the teeth of the iguana lizard.

- **In the late 1830s,** British scientist Richard Owen realized that some fossils did not belong to lizards, but to an as yet unnamed group of reptiles.

- **In 1841–1842,** Richard Owen invented a new name for the group of giant prehistoric reptiles—Dinosauria.

- **The name "dinosaur"** means "terrible reptile."

- **Life-sized models** of several dinosaurs were made by sculptor Waterhouse Hawkins in 1852–1854.

- **Hawkins' models** were displayed in the gardens of the Crystal Palace Exhibition in London, and caused a public sensation—the first wave of "Dino-mania."

- **The three main dinosaurs** of the Dinosauria in the 1840s were *Iguanodon*, the big meat eater *Megalosaurus,* and the nodosaur *Hyelosaurus.*

◀ *Even though* Iguanodon *is now one of the best-known dinosaurs, it confused paleontologists when its fossils were first discovered. They thought that its distinctive thumb claw belonged on its nose!* Megalosaurus, *a very early discovery, was the first dinosaur to be given an official scientific name, even though the term "dinosaur" (meaning "terrible reptile") was not invented until 1841.*

205

Recreating dinosaurs

▶ *A mosquito perfectly preserved in amber is a reminder that many other creatures lived during the time of the dinosaurs. Recreating them, however, is beyond today's science.*

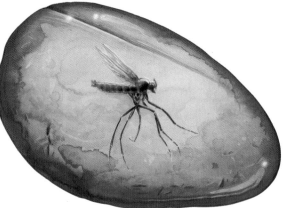

- **The *Jurassic Park* movies** showed dinosaurs being recreated as living creatures in the modern world.

- **The instructions**, or genes, of all animals, including dinosaurs, are in the form of the genetic substance known as DNA (deoxyribonucleic acid).

- **In *Jurassic Park,*** dinosaur DNA came not from dinosaur fossils, but from mosquitoes that had sucked the blood of living dinosaurs, and then been preserved in solidified amber.

- **Scientists** in *Jurassic Park* combined the DNA of dinosaurs with DNA from living amphibians such as frogs.

- **Tiny bits of DNA** have been recovered from fossils formed in the Age of Dinosaurs.

- **The bits of dinosaur DNA found so far** represent a tiny amount of the DNA needed to recreate a living thing.

- **Most scientists** doubt that living dinosaurs could really be made from bits of fossilized DNA.

▲ *The heroes of the movie* Jurassic Park *come face to face with a pack of* Velociraptors, *which actually lived during the Upper Cretaceous Period, about 80-84 million years ago.*

- **Plants today** might not be suited to "modern" dinosaurs.

- **"Modern" dinosaurs** might die from today's diseases.

- **The task of recreating** a living dinosaur from tiny fragments of DNA has been compared to writing all the plays of Shakespeare starting with a couple of words.

207

Index

Index

Index

Index

Index

Index

Index

Index

Acknowledgments

The publishers would like to thank the following artists who have contributed to this book:

Andy Beckett, Chris Buzer (Galante Studio),
Steve Caldwell, Alan Hancocks, Stuart Lafford,
Kevin Maddison, Alan Male (Linden Artists),
Maltings, Janos Marffy, Alessandro Menchi
(Galante Studio), Steve Roberts, Martin Sanders,
Rudi Visi, Steve Weston, Mike White

The publishers would like to thank the following sources for the use of their photographs:

Science Pictures Limited/Corbis: Page 16, page 171
Kobal Collection/Amblin/Universal: Page 207

All other pictures from the Miles Kelly Archives, Corbis
Professional Collections, Corel Corporation, PhotoDisk